pizza
& focaccia

pizza
& focaccia

simple recipes for delicious food every day

LONDON · NEW YORK

Senior Designer Toni Kay

Senior Production Controller
Toby Marshall

Art Director Leslie Harrington

Editorial Director Julia Charles

Indexer Hilary Bird

First published in 2013
by Ryland Peters & Small
20–21 Jockey's Fields
London WC1R 4BW
and
519 Broadway, 5th Floor
New York NY 10012

www.rylandpeters.com

Text © Maxine Clark, Annie Rigg, Ross Dobson,
Fiona Beckett, Isidora Popovic, Silvana Franca
and Ryland Peters & Small 2013

Design and photographs © Ryland Peters & Small
2013

ISBN: 978-1-84975-379-1

10 9 8 7 6 5 4 3 2 1

US Library of Congress Cataloging-in-Publication
data has been applied for.

Printed and bound in China

notes:
• All spoon measurements are level, unless
otherwise specified.
• Ovens should be preheated to the specified
temperature. Recipes in this book were tested
using a regular oven. If using a fan-assisted
oven, follow the manufacturer's instructions
for adjusting temperatures.
• All eggs are medium UK/large US, unless
otherwise specified. Recipes containing raw
or partially cooked egg should not be served
to the very young, very old, anyone with a
compromised immune system or pregnant
women.

contents

introduction

Pizza is said to have originated on the streets of Naples, to feed and fill ordinary working people cheaply. Its roots are distinctly southern Italian, and pizza is considered a food of the city. Pizza alla Napoletana is always 'open pizza' (never filled, folded and baked). However, the way to eat pizza in the street is to fold it in quarters, hold it in a napkin and munch it like a sandwich. The Associazione Vera Pizza Napoletana lays down strict rules for the making and cooking of pizza in order to be able to sell it as Pizza Napoletana. Little stuffed and deep-fried pizzelle and panzerotti are other examples of street food from Naples and Campania. In Rome, pizza is sold by the metre (or its parts). Throughout Italy, other types of flat hearth breads, such as focaccia and schiacciata, were traditionally made at home on the hot hearth where the embers had been.

The only ingredients necessary to make pizza dough are flour, salt, yeast and water. Adding olive oil gives a good texture and flavour to the dough when baked at home. Salt will bring the flavour out of the dough and strengthen the crust but if you are using a flaky sea or crystal salt, make sure it is finely ground, or dissolve it in the warm water before adding it to the flour. Any type of yeast you are happy with will do – just follow the manufacturer's instructions, using the liquid specified in the recipe. As for water, the softer the water, the better the dough, so use filtered water or even bottled water in hard water areas. Focaccia relies on olive oil for flavour, so you must use extra virgin olive oil. It doesn't have to be an expensive one – a supermarket blend of extra virgin olive oils will do. Always anoint your piping hot pizza with extra virgin olive oil (flavoured or not) before you eat it. Not only will it look better, it will also taste sublime!

The best advice to any novice pizza-maker is to keep the choice of topping as simple as possible to truly appreciate the flavours. The crust is all-important and turns soggy if it is weighed down too much. Slice meat and vegetables thinly and don't smother the base with too much sauce or cheese. Most important of all, eat it hot, hot, hot, straight out of the oven. So go on, get your hands in some dough right now and bake a fragrant pizza or focaccia. You don't need to buy any special ingredients – just start off with an olive oil, salt and garlic topping and savour your first homemade pizza.

basics equipment and utensils

Making pizza dough couldn't be easier, and when you become familiar with the process, you can guess the quantities by eye. To make really good pizza, you will need a few basic items in the kitchen, the most important being your hands!

You should have a good selection of the usual suspects: **mixing bowls**, **measuring spoons, measuring jugs, weighing scales** or **cup measures**; a good **sharp knife** or **pastry wheel** for cutting dough; a **large serrated knife** for cutting focaccia.

A very useful gadget is a **pastry scraper** which can be used as a knife, scoop and board scraper or cleaner. Scrapers come in all guises but they usually comprise a rectangular metal 'blade', one edge of which is covered by a wooden or plastic handle that fits into the palm of your hand.

If you are really serious about pizza-making and want to make dough in quantity, an **electric food mixer** will take the pain out of mixing and kneading large batches of dough, although there's nothing quite as satisfying as hand-kneading a big, soft pillow of dough.

Clingfilm/plastic wrap is the modern alternative to a damp tea towel. This is used to cover a dough when it is rising to keep it moist and to stop the surface drying out and forming a crust, which can impair the rising. On its own it will stick to a dough, so either lightly rub the dough with a little olive oil, or spray or brush the clingfilm lightly with oil before covering the dough. Alternatively, cover the rising dough with a large, upturned mixing bowl.

Non-stick baking parchment is a revelation for making pizza. There is no need to dust the bottom of the pizza with masses of extra flour (which never cooks) to prevent it sticking. Dusting with cornmeal is in no way authentic and it sticks to the dough, ruining the texture.

A good, steady work surface at the right height is essential for energetic kneading. The surface should be able to cope with sticky dough, flour and olive oil and should be easy to clean.

A **flour sifter** or **shaker** is useful as it will limit the flour you sprinkle onto the dough and is always to hand. Alternatively, you can make do with a little bowl of extra flour on the side, for dusting.

An **olive-oil pourer** will allow you to drizzle small amounts of olive oil onto a pizza or into a dough. Some are cans with long spouts, and some neatly fit into the olive-oil bottle itself.

A **water spray** mists a dough with just enough water to keep it moist.

Pastry brushes are always handy, especially when brushing the calzone with oil or water and for brushing the edges of dough before sealing.

Biscuit cutters will cut dough into smaller shapes for stuffing or filling.

You will need one or two **deep, heavy metal pans/pizza pans/springform cake pans** for deep-pan pizzas and focaccias; **heavy rectangular pans** and **lipped baking sheets** for larger pizzas; and good, heavy, rimless **baking sheets** (or turn them upside down) for baking pizzas and to act as pizza peels or paddles to shoot the pizza into the oven. Pans with a non-stick surface tend to 'stew' doughs – I prefer metal, iron or heavy aluminium. Never use the large pans with perforated bases to make fresh pizzas – these are specifically for reheating bought pizzas and do not work with fresh dough.

Pizza peels or **paddles** are a luxury, but lovely to have and very functional. Wooden peels can act as a serving dish. Metal peels are more practical, although they heat up when they go in and out of the oven and this can make the dough stick to them.

Pizza wheels slice efficiently through a hot pizza without dragging off all the topping.

A *testo* or **bakestone** is an affordable luxury if you don't have that outdoor, wood-fired pizza oven. Preheated in the oven for at least 30 minutes before starting to bake, the stone mimics the base of a real pizza oven, and when the uncooked pizza comes into contact with the stone, the moisture is absorbed, the heat evenly distributed and the base will crisp up nicely. There are all types from round to rectangular on the market – some ovens have them as an optional extra. Thick, unglazed quarry/terracotta tiles are a good alternative – use them to line a shelf in the oven. They can be any size, as long as they fit together.

Pizza can be made very successfully in all types of ovens, but you will get the best results at home if you have a **standard electric oven** which can reach temperatures of more than 200°C (400°F) Gas 6, and ideally, 220°C (425°F) Gas 7. This will cook the base quickly and be as close to the real thing as possible. Although fan-assisted ovens will work for pizza- and focaccia-baking, they tend to dry out the crust before it browns and the crust can be very pale.

A **wood-burning oven** is the ultimate for the serious pizza aficionado. It will heat to the right temperature and give that all-important smoky taste, which comes from the burning wood. A pizza cooked in one of these will take just minutes as the temperature is more than 500°C (930°F). Domestic ovens are available and could end up being your best friend!

ten pizza pointers

yeast

Whatever yeast you use, it needs moisture and warmth to develop. Make sure the liquid is at the correct temperature – too cold and the dough will rise slowly; too hot and you risk killing the yeast. When a recipe states 'hand-hot water', it should be between 40.5°C (105°F) and 46°C (115°F).

flour

Using fine Italian '0' grade flour gives the best domestic results. Finer '00' grade is used by professionals and will not give a robust crust at home. Unbleached white bread flour, a mix of soft and hard wheats, will give a very good crust. If you are making dough in a hurry, warm the flour in the microwave for 10 seconds before adding the other ingredients. Always have surplus flour on hand to dust your dough, hands, rolling pin and work surface.

dough

When making the dough, remember: the wetter the dough, the better the dough. A stiff, firm dough is difficult to knead and even more difficult to shape. It will have a poor texture and will not rise properly. If kneaded well, the stickiness soon disappears. Always have olive oil on hand for oiling clingfilm/plastic wrap, dough, bowls and pans, if required, to stop the dough from sticking.

kneading

If the dough sticks to your hands when kneading, stop and quickly wash your hands then dip them in a little flour to dry them. You will find the dough doesn't stick to clean hands. Kneading should stretch the dough and develop the elastic gluten in the flour – don't be shy in pulling and stretching the dough.

shaping

Starting off with a perfect round ball will make stretching the dough into a circle much easier. Shape each one into a smooth ball and place on a well-floured tea towel to rise. Dredge liberally all over with flour. When risen, flip the balls over onto a work surface (the flour will have stuck to the dough giving it a non-stick base) and roll out.

topping

The cardinal sin in pizza-making is to overwhelm perfectly-made dough with too much topping. This can make it difficult to shoot into the oven and prevents it rising. If any topping drips down the side of the pizza, making it wet, it will not rise. Cheese that misses the target will melt and glue the pizza to the bakestone or parchment.

base

If you like pizzas with a good crisp base, and make them often, it is worth investing in a porous bakestone or *testo*. Some ovens have them as an accessory, but they are cheap to buy. Otherwise a large, heavy baking sheet that will not warp will do. If you have a solid-fuel oven, cook pizzas directly on the base of the hot oven.

baking

The best way to get a pizza into the oven is to roll the dough directly onto non-stick baking parchment and slide this onto a rimless baking sheet or pizza peel. It will then slide onto the preheated *testo* or baking sheet easily. For the best results, quickly slide out the parchment paper from under the pizza 5 minutes after the pizza has 'set'. This will make sure that the base crisps up.

serving

Always serve a pizza as soon as it is cooked, slip it onto a wooden board and cut it using a pizza wheel, as knives can drag the topping. Leave filled pizzas to cool for 5 minutes before eating as they can burn the mouth!

eating

Pizza is best eaten in the hand – the crust is there to act as a handle! In Naples, pizzas are folded in four and eaten like a huge sandwich in a paper napkin. Eating it with a knife and fork just sends it skimming across the plate!

basic pizza dough

25 g/1 cake fresh/compressed yeast, 1 tablespoon/1 packet dried active baking yeast or 2 teaspoons fast-action/quick-rising dried yeast

½ teaspoon sugar

250 ml/1 cup hand-hot water

500 g/4 cups unbleached white bread flour or Italian '0' flour, plus extra to dust

1 teaspoon fine sea salt

1 tablespoon olive oil

Makes 2 medium-crust pizzas, 25–30 cm/10–12 inches

This will make the typical Neapolitan pizza – soft and chewy with a crisp crust or *cornicione*.

In a medium bowl, cream the fresh/compressed yeast with the sugar and whisk in the hand-hot water. Leave for 10 minutes until frothy. For other yeasts, follow the manufacturer's instructions.

Sift the flour and salt into a large bowl and make a well in the centre. Pour in the yeast mixture, then the olive oil. Mix together with a round-bladed knife, then use your hands until the dough comes together. Tip out onto a lightly floured surface, wash and dry your hands, then knead briskly for 5–10 minutes until smooth, shiny and elastic. (5 minutes for warm hands, 10 minutes for cold hands!) Don't add extra flour at this stage – a wetter dough is better. If you feel the dough is sticky, flour your hands, not the dough. The dough should be quite soft. If it is *really* too soft, knead in a little more flour.

To test if the dough is ready, roll it into a fat sausage, take each end in either hand, lift the dough up and stretch it outwards, gently wiggling it up and down – it should stretch out quite easily. If it doesn't, it needs more kneading. Shape the dough into a neat ball. Put in an oiled bowl, cover with clingfilm/plastic wrap or a damp tea towel and leave to rise in a warm, draught-free place until doubled in size – about 1½ hours.

Uncover the dough, punch out the air, then tip out onto a lightly floured work surface. Divide into 2 and shape into smooth balls. Place the balls well apart on non-stick baking parchment, cover loosely with clingfilm and leave to rise for 60–90 minutes. Use as desired.

Sicilian pizza dough

10 g/½ cake fresh/compressed yeast, 1 teaspoon dried active baking yeast or ½ teaspoon fast-action/quick-rising dried yeast

a pinch of sugar

150 ml/⅔ cup hand-hot water

250 g/2 cups fine semolina flour (*farina di semola*) or durum wheat flour

½ teaspoon fine sea salt

1 tablespoon olive oil

1 tablespoon freshly squeezed lemon juice

Makes 2 thin-crust pizzas, 20–25 cm/8–10 inches

Sicilians tend to use the indigenous yellow *farina di semola* (hard wheat flour), which ensures a lighter crust, with lemon juice to add to the lightness and strengthen the dough.

In a medium bowl, cream the fresh/compressed yeast with the sugar and whisk in the hand-hot water. Leave for 10 minutes until frothy. For other yeasts, follow the manufacturer's instructions.

Sift the flour and salt into a large bowl and make a well in the centre. Pour in the yeast mixture, olive oil and lemon juice. Mix until the dough comes together. Add more water if necessary – the dough should be very soft. Tip out onto a lightly floured surface, wash and dry your hands, then knead briskly for at least 10 minutes until smooth, shiny and elastic. It takes longer to knead this type of dough. Don't add extra flour at this stage – a wetter dough is better. If you feel the dough is sticky, flour your hands, not the dough. The dough should be quite soft. If it is really too soft, knead in a little more flour.

To test if the dough is ready, roll it into a fat sausage, take each end in either hand, lift the dough up and stretch it outwards, gently wiggling it up and down – it should stretch out quite easily. If it doesn't, it needs more kneading. Shape the dough into a neat ball. Put in an oiled bowl, cover with clingfilm/plastic wrap or a damp tea towel and leave to rise in a warm, draught-free place until doubled in size – about 1½ hours.

Uncover the dough, punch out the air, then tip out onto a lightly floured work surface. Divide into 2 and shape into smooth balls. Place the balls well apart on non-stick baking parchment, cover loosely with clingfilm and leave to rise for 60–90 minutes. Use as desired.

basic focaccia

750 g/6⅓ cups Italian '00' flour or plain/all-purpose flour, plus extra to dust

25 g/1 cake fresh/compressed yeast, 1 tablespoon dried active baking yeast or 2 teaspoons fast-action/quick-rising dried yeast

150 ml/⅔ cup extra virgin olive oil

425–500 ml/1¾–2 cups hand-hot water

coarse sea salt, to sprinkle

fresh rosemary sprigs (optional)

2 x 25-cm/10-inch cake pans

Makes 2 focaccias, 25 cm/10 inches

Focaccias are found in many different guises all over Italy, and can be thin and crisp, thick and soft, round or square. This basic one has been baked in a round pan, but it can be made in any shape you wish. You can leave out the rosemary, or use different toppings.

Sift the flour and fine sea salt into a large bowl and make a well in the centre. Crumble in the fresh/compressed yeast. For other yeasts, follow the manufacturer's instructions. Pour in 6 tablespoons of the olive oil, then rub in the yeast until the mixture resembles fine breadcrumbs. Pour in the water and mix with your hands until the dough comes together.

Tip the dough out onto a floured surface, wash and dry your hands, and knead energetically for 10 minutes until smooth and elastic. The dough should be almost too soft to handle, but don't worry about that at this stage. Put it in a lightly oiled bowl, cover with clingfilm/plastic wrap or a damp tea towel and leave to rise in a warm place until doubled in size – about 1½ hours.

Lightly oil two 25-cm/10-inch cake pans. Uncover the dough, punch out the air and divide in 2. Shape each piece into a round ball on a lightly floured surface, roll out into two 25-cm/10-inch circles and place in the pans. Cover with clingfilm or a damp tea towel and leave to rise for 30 minutes.

Uncover the dough. Push your fingertips into the dough right down to the base of the pan (don't overdo it!), to make deep dimples all over the surface. The dough will deflate slightly. Drizzle very generously with about 80 ml/⅓ cup olive oil so that the dimples contain little pools of delicious oil.

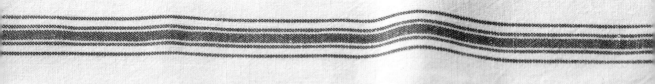

Top with little sprigs of rosemary leaves, if using, and a generous sprinkling of salt. Re-cover with clingfilm or a damp tea towel and leave the dough to rise to the top of the pans – about 30 minutes. Preheat the oven to 200°C (400°F) Gas 6.

Spray the focaccias with water and bake for 20–25 minutes until risen and golden. Drizzle with the remaining olive oil, then transfer to a wire rack to cool. Eat on the same day or leave to cool, then wrap and freeze. To reheat, thaw, then wrap in aluminium foil and heat in a hot oven for 5 minutes.

sauces

salsa pizzaiola

This is a key ingredient of pizza and gives it its distinctive flavour. It is a speciality of Naples, but is quite common throughout Italy. To acquire its concentrated, almost caramelized flavour, the tomatoes must be fried over a lively heat.

8 tablespoons/½ cup olive oil

2 garlic cloves, chopped

1 teaspoon dried oregano

2 x 400-g/14-oz. cans chopped tomatoes (drained and juice reserved) or 800 g/2 lb. fresh tomatoes, halved and cored

sea salt and freshly ground black pepper

Makes about 400 ml/1¾ cups

In a large, shallow pan, heat the oil almost to smoking point (a wok is good for this).

Standing back to avoid the spluttering, add the garlic, oregano and tomatoes including the reserved canned tomato juice (if using). Cook over a fierce heat for 5–8 minutes or until the sauce is thick and glossy. Season.

Pass the sauce through a food mill (mouli) set over a bowl, to remove seeds and skin. You can put the smooth sauce back in the pan to reduce further if you like. Ladle the sauce into the centre of the pizza base and spread it out in a circular motion with the back of a ladle.

classic pesto genovese

2 garlic cloves

50 g/½ cup pine nuts

2 big handfuls fresh basil leaves

150 ml/⅔ cup extra virgin olive oil, plus extra to preserve

50 g/3 tablespoons unsalted butter, softened

4 tablespoons freshly grated Parmesan cheese

sea salt and freshly ground black pepper

Makes about 250 ml/1 cup

Peel the garlic and put it in a pestle and mortar with a little salt and the pine nuts. Pound until broken up. Add the basil leaves, a few at a time, pounding and mixing to a paste. Gradually beat in the olive oil, little by little, until the mixture is creamy and thick.

Beat in the butter and season with pepper, then beat in the Parmesan. Spoon into a screw-top jar with a layer of olive oil on top to exclude the air, then store in the fridge for up to 2 weeks, until needed.

fiery red pesto

1 large red pepper

2 big handfuls fresh basil leaves

1 garlic clove

30 g/⅓ cup toasted pine nuts

6 sun-dried tomatoes in oil, drained

2 ripe tomatoes, skinned

3 tablespoons tomato purée/paste

½ teaspoon chilli powder

50 g/½ cup freshly grated Parmesan cheese

150 ml/⅔ cup olive oil, plus extra to preserve

Makes about 350 ml/1½ cups

Preheat the grill/broiler to high.

Place the pepper on the grill rack and grill/broil, turning occasionally, until charred all over. Put the pepper in a covered bowl until cool enough to handle, then peel off the skin. Halve and remove the core and seeds.

Place the pepper and the remaining ingredients, except the oil, in a food processor. Process until smooth, then, with the machine running, slowly add the oil. Spoon into a screw-top jar with a layer of olive oil on top to exclude the air, then store in the fridge for up to 2 weeks, until needed.

black olive and tomato relish

2 tablespoons sun-dried tomato oil

1 red onion, peeled and diced

1 garlic clove, peeled and crushed

5 plump sun-dried tomatoes in oil, drained and diced

250 g/8 oz. pitted black (or oven-dried) olives

1 fresh bay leaf

15 fresh basil leaves, torn into pieces

freshly squeezed juice of 1 lemon

3–4 tablespoons extra virgin olive oil, plus extra to preserve

sea salt and freshly ground black pepper

Makes about 350 g (1½ cups)

In a medium saucepan, heat the sun-dried tomato oil and gently sweat the onion and garlic for a few minutes. Add the sun-dried tomatoes, olives and bay leaf and continue to cook for a few minutes until the flavours have melded.

Season, remove from the heat and discard the bay leaf. Pour the mixture into a food processor with the basil and process to a coarse purée. Add the lemon juice and oil. Season, if needed. Spoon into a screw-top jar with a layer of olive oil to exclude the air, then store in the fridge for up to 2 weeks, until needed.

These are wonderfully useful sauces and relishes to have on hand in the fridge to spread on pizza dough or serve with flatbreads as a dip. Don't stint on the fresh herbs.

Here you'll find a delicious collection of the best pizza recipes. Many of them will be familiar to you from pizzeria menus, such as the ever-popular Margherita, and others less so, as they are regional specialities enjoyed in Italy.

pizzas, thick and thin

The recipe for this basic pizza dough originated in Sicily. Using a touch of lemon juice in the dough (usually made with special finely ground semolina flour for making bread, pasta and pizzas) makes it light and crisp. Adapt this recipe to ordinary plain/all-purpose flour and it works very well, but the crust is not as golden. This is a very patriotic pizza – the three colours representing the Italian flag.

pizza margherita

250 g/2 cups fine Italian semolina flour or plain/all-purpose flour

7g/¼ oz. fresh/compressed yeast

1 tablespoon lemon juice

1 tablespoon extra virgin olive oil

a pinch of sea salt

about 300 ml/1¼ cups warm water

Pizza topping

1 recipe Salsa Pizzaiola (page 18)

250-g/9-oz ball fresh mozzarella cheese, thinly sliced

a handful of fresh basil leaves

extra good olive oil, for drizzling

salt and freshly ground black pepper

2 large, heavy baking sheets lined with non-stick baking parchment

Makes 2 thin-crust pizzas, 23 cm/9 inches

Put the baking sheets in the oven and preheat to 220°C (425°F) Gas 7.

To make the dough, put the flour in a bowl, crumble the fresh yeast into the flour, add the lemon juice, olive oil and a generous pinch of salt, then add enough warm water to form a very soft dough. Transfer to a floured surface and knead for 10 minutes or until smooth and elastic. Put the dough in a clean, oiled bowl, cover and let rise for about 1 hour, until doubled in size.

Cut the dough in half and knead each half into a round. Pat or roll the rounds into 23-cm/9-inch circles, keeping the bases well floured. Transfer the pizzas onto the baking sheets lined with non-stick baking parchment. Spread each one lightly with salsa pizzaiola, cover with sliced mozzarella and season with salt and pepper. Let rise in a warm place for 10 minutes, then open the oven door, and slide paper and pizza onto the hot baking sheets. If you are brave, try to shoot them into the oven so that they leave the paper behind – this takes practice!

Bake for 18–20 minutes, until the crust is golden and the cheese melted but still white. Remove from the oven, sprinkle with basil leaves and olive oil, then eat immediately.

Pizza dough

150 g/1¼ cups strong white bread flour

125 g/1 cup Italian '00' flour

1 teaspoon fine sea salt

1 teaspoon fast-acting/quick rising yeast

½ teaspoon sugar

2 tablespoons olive oil, plus extra to drizzle

about 175 ml/¾ cup hand-hot water

semolina or cornmeal, to dust the baking trays

Pizza topping

400 ml/1⅔ cups good-quality passata

150 g/5 oz. Pecorino Toscano (rind removed), sliced

150 g/5 oz. Taleggio (rind removed) or buffalo mozzarella, sliced

90 g/3 oz. Gorgonzola piccante, crumbled

30 g/⅓ cup freshly grated mature Parmesan

a small handful of fresh oregano or basil leaves

freshly ground black pepper

2 large baking sheets, lightly oiled

Makes 2 pizzas

irresistible Italian four-cheese pizza

If you always reject the pizza *quattro formaggi* as being bland and indigestible, just try making it with top-quality Italian cheeses.

To make the pizza dough, sift the 2 flours into a bowl along with the salt, yeast and sugar. Mix together, then form a hollow in the centre. Add the olive oil and half the hand-hot water and stir to incorporate the flour. Gradually add as much of the remaining water as you need to pull the dough together. (It should take most of it – you need a wettish dough.) Turn the dough out onto a board and knead for 10 minutes until smooth and elastic, adding a little extra flour to prevent the dough sticking if necessary. Put the dough into a lightly oiled bowl, cover with clingfilm/plastic wrap and leave in a warm place until doubled in size, about 1–1¼ hours.

Preheat the oven to 240°C (475°F) Gas 9 and sprinkle the prepared baking trays with semolina.

Tip the dough out of the bowl and press down on it to knock out the air. Divide it in half. Pull and shape one piece of dough into a large circle, then place it on a prepared baking tray and push it out towards the edges of the tray. (It doesn't have to be a perfect circle!) Spread half the passata over the top, then arrange half the cheeses over the top. Season with pepper. Repeat with the other piece of dough and the remaining cheese. Drizzle a little olive oil over the top of each pizza and bake in the preheated oven for 8–10 minutes until the dough has puffed up and the cheese is brown and bubbling. Garnish the pizzas with oregano leaves and drizzle over a little more oil.

This is *the* classic pizza and it is always made without mozzarella. According to Neapolitans, when anchovies are added, it is transformed into a Pizza Romana. Dried oregano is preferable to fresh, as it is much more fragrant, especially if you crush it between your fingers before sprinkling over the pizza. In Italy, wild oregano is sold in thick bunches, dries out in a matter of days and is rubbed straight off the bunch into whatever's cooking.

pizza marinara

½ recipe Basic Pizza Dough (page 13), making just 1 ball of dough

3–4 tablespoons Pizzaiola Sauce (page 18)

2 or 3 very ripe tomatoes, sliced and deseeded

2 garlic cloves, thinly sliced

1 teaspoon dried oregano

extra virgin olive oil, to drizzle

a few sprigs fresh oregano

sea salt and freshly ground black pepper

a testo, terracotta bakestone or a large, heavy baking sheet

a pizza peel or rimless baking sheet

Makes 1 medium-crust pizza, 25–35 cm/10–14 inches

Put the testo, terracotta bakestone or a large, heavy baking sheet on the lower shelf of the oven. Preheat the oven to 220°C (425°F) Gas 7 for at least 30 minutes.

Uncover the dough, punch out the air and roll or pull into a 25-cm circle directly onto non-stick baking parchment. Slide this onto the pizza peel or rimless baking sheet. Spread the pizzaiola sauce over the pizza base, leaving a 1-cm rim around the edge. Scatter with the tomatoes and garlic, sprinkle with the dried oregano, drizzle with olive oil, then season.

Working quickly, open the oven door and slide paper and pizza onto the hot bakestone or baking sheet. If you are brave, try to shoot the pizza into the oven so that it leaves the paper behind – this takes practice!

Bake for 5 minutes, then carefully slide out the baking parchment. Bake the pizza for a further 15 minutes, or until the crust is golden. Remove from the oven, scatter with the fresh oregano and drizzle with olive oil. Eat immediately.

½ recipe Basic Pizza Dough
(page 13), making just 1 ball
of dough

50–75 g/2–3 oz. buffalo
mozzarella or cow's milk
mozzarella (*fior di latte*)

200 g/about 6 plum tomatoes,
halved

150 g/5 oz. fresh spicy sausage,
sliced or removed from the skin
and crumbled

50 g/2 oz. Peppadew peppers

½ teaspoon fennel seeds

red chilli flakes, to taste

chilli oil or extra virgin olive oil,
to drizzle

sea salt and freshly ground
black pepper

*a testo, terracotta bakestone
or a large, heavy baking sheet*

*a pizza peel or rimless
baking sheet*

**Makes 1 medium-crust pizza,
25–35 cm/10–14 inches**

This is quite a substantial pizza, and can be as fiery and angry
(*arrabiata*) as you like – it's up to you how much chilli you put in.
This is delicious made with fresh Italian sausage meat, but you
could use thick slices of salame piccante or even a hot merguez
or chorizo. Chilled beer is an essential accompaniment.

pizza arrabiata

Put the testo, terracotta bakestone or a large, heavy baking sheet on
the lower shelf of the oven. Preheat the oven to 220°C (425°F) Gas 7
for at least 30 minutes.

Uncover the dough, punch out the air and roll or pull into a 25-cm/10-
inch circle directly onto non-stick baking parchment. Slide this onto the
pizza peel or rimless baking sheet. Spread the pizzaiola sauce over the
pizza base, leaving a 1-cm/½-inch rim around the edge. Scatter with the
tomatoes and garlic, sprinkle with the dried oregano, drizzle with olive oil,
then season.

Working quickly, open the oven door and slide paper and pizza onto the
hot bakestone or baking sheet. If you are brave, try to shoot the pizza
into the oven so that it leaves the paper behind – this takes practice!

Bake for 5 minutes, then carefully slide out the baking parchment. Bake
the pizza for a further 15 minutes, or until the crust is golden. Remove
from the oven, scatter with the fresh oregano and drizzle with olive oil.
Eat immediately.

pizza bianca

½ recipe Basic Pizza Dough (page 13), making just 1 ball of dough

100 g/3½ oz. buffalo mozzarella or cow's milk mozzarella (*fior di latte*)

a handful of small fresh sage leaves

extra virgin olive oil, to drizzle

sea salt and freshly ground black pepper

a testo, terracotta bakestone or a large, heavy baking sheet

a pizza peel or rimless baking sheet

Makes 1 medium-crust pizza, 25–35 cm/10–14 inches

Neapolitans naturally call pizza without tomatoes *pizza bianca* ('white pizza'). All the flavour comes from the cheese, so it has to be the finest buffalo mozzarella. This tends to be quite wet, so squeeze out any watery whey before slicing it. Try adding sage to the pizza – its muskiness beautifully complements the milky mozzarella.

Put the testo, terracotta bakestone or a large, heavy baking sheet on the lower shelf of the oven. Preheat the oven to 220°C (425°F) Gas 7 for at least 30 minutes.

Lightly squeeze any excess moisture out of the mozzarella, then slice it and put it on kitchen paper for 5 minutes to absorb any remaining moisture.

Uncover the dough, punch out the air and roll or pull into a 25-cm/10-inch circle directly onto non-stick baking parchment. Slide this onto the pizza peel or rimless baking sheet. Arrange the mozzarella evenly over the pizza base, leaving a 1-cm/½-inch rim around the edge. Scatter the sage over the cheese, then season and drizzle with olive oil.

Working quickly, open the oven door and slide paper and pizza onto the hot bakestone or baking sheet. If you are brave, try to shoot the pizza into the oven so that it leaves the paper behind – this takes practice!

Bake for 5 minutes, then carefully slide out the baking parchment. Bake the pizza for a further 15 minutes, or until the crust is golden and the cheese melted and bubbling. Remove from the oven and sprinkle with freshly ground black pepper. Eat immediately.

garlic mushroom pizza

½ recipe Basic Pizza Dough (page 13), making just 1 ball of dough

50–75 g/2–3 oz. buffalo mozzarella or cow's milk mozzarella (*fior di latte*)

50 g/½ cup fresh breadcrumbs

30 g/¼ cup freshly grated Parmesan cheese

4 garlic cloves, finely chopped

4 tablespoons chopped fresh parsley

30 g/2 tablespoons butter, melted

about 12 medium chestnut/cremini mushrooms

extra virgin olive oil, to drizzle

sea salt and freshly ground black pepper

a testo, terracotta bakestone or a large, heavy baking sheet

a pizza peel or rimless baking sheet

Makes 1 medium-crust pizza, 25–35 cm/10–14 inches

This makes a change from the normal scattering of token sliced mushrooms: here we have fresh mushrooms in all their glory, under a crispy garlicky topping of breadcrumbs and Parmesan. Don't use white mushrooms for this – they often have little or no taste at all. Chestnut/cremini or other large, dark open mushrooms are ideal.

Put the testo, terracotta bakestone or a large, heavy baking sheet on the lower shelf of the oven. Preheat the oven to 220°C (425°F) Gas 7 for at least 30 minutes.

Lightly squeeze any excess moisture out of the mozzarella, then slice or chop into cubes. Mix the breadcrumbs with the Parmesan, garlic and parsley, then stir in the melted butter. Lightly fill the cavities of the mushrooms with the breadcrumb mixture.

Uncover the dough, punch out the air and roll or pull into a 25-cm/10-inch circle directly onto non-stick baking parchment. Slide this onto the pizza peel or rimless baking sheet. Arrange the mozzarella over the pizza base leaving a 2-cm/1-inch rim around the edge. Arrange the stuffed mushrooms all over, sprinkling any remaining breadcrumbs over the finished pizza. Drizzle with olive oil and season.

Working quickly, open the oven door and slide paper and pizza onto the hot bakestone or baking sheet. If you are brave, try to shoot the pizza into the oven so that it leaves the paper behind – this takes practice!

Bake for 5 minutes, then slide out the baking parchment if possible (this will be quite difficult with the wobbly mushrooms). Bake for a further 15 minutes or until the crust is golden, the cheese melted and the mushrooms tender and bubbling. Remove from the oven and drizzle with olive oil. Eat immediately.

With no hint of tomato sauce, this is a succulent pizza where the onions are cooked until soft and caramelized, before being spread on the pizza on top of the mozzarella. Olives, capers and anchovies add savouriness to the sweet onions. You may leave out the anchovies and add tuna or sardines instead.

caramelized red onion pizza with capers and olives

1 recipe Basic Pizza Dough (page 13), dividing the dough into 6–8 balls

1 kg/2¼ lb. red onions, finely sliced

freshly squeezed juice of 1 lemon

4 tablespoons olive oil, plus extra to drizzle

2 teaspoons dried oregano

1 mozzarella, drained and thinly sliced

2 tablespoons freshly grated Parmesan cheese

12 anchovy fillets in oil, drained (optional)

15 black olives, pitted

2 tablespoons capers in salt, washed and drained

sea salt and freshly ground black pepper

two testi, terracotta bakestones or large, heavy baking sheets

2 rimless baking sheets

Makes 6–8 pizzas, depending on size

Put the testi, terracotta bakestones or large, heavy baking sheets on the lower shelf of the oven. Preheat the oven to 220°C (425°F) Gas 7 for at least 30 minutes.

Toss the onions in the lemon juice to coat them thoroughly. Heat the oil in a large, shallow saucepan and add the onions. Cook over a gentle heat for about 10 minutes, stirring occasionally, until they are beginning to colour. Stir in the dried oregano.

Uncover the dough balls, punch out the air and roll or pull each one into thin circles directly onto separate sheets of non-stick baking parchment. Slide these onto 2 rimless baking sheets.

Cover the pizza bases with the mozzarella leaving a 1-cm/½-inch rim around the edge. Top with the onions and sprinkle with the Parmesan. Scatter the anchovy fillets, olives and capers over the top. Drizzle with olive oil, then season, but don't use too much salt as the capers will be salty.

Working quickly, open the oven door, and slide paper and pizzas onto the hot bakestones or baking sheets. Bake for 15–20 minutes or until the crust is golden. Remove from the oven and drizzle with olive oil. Eat immediately.

350 g/13 oz. young spinach leaves

1 tablespoon butter

2 garlic cloves, crushed

1 recipe Basic Pizza Dough (page 13)

1–2 tablespoons olive oil

½ recipe Salsa Pizzaiola (page 18)

150 g/5 oz. mozzarella cheese, drained and thinly sliced

4 small eggs

50 g/½ cup finely grated fontina or Gruyère cheese

sea salt and freshly ground black pepper

a testo, terracotta bakestone or a large, heavy baking sheet

Makes 4 small pizzas

pizza fiorentina

Spinach and egg pizzas are a favourite in pizza restaurants everywhere, and you can easily make them at home. It doesn't matter if the yolk is a bit hard, but make sure it goes onto the pizza whole.

Put a testo, bakestone or baking sheet in the oven and preheat the oven to 220°C (425°F) Gas 7.

Wash the spinach thoroughly and put into a large saucepan. Cover with a lid and cook for 2–3 minutes, until the spinach wilts. Drain well and, when the spinach is cool enough to handle, squeeze out any excess water with your hands.

Melt the butter in a frying pan and cook the garlic for 1 minute. Add the drained spinach and cook for a further 3–4 minutes. Add salt and pepper to taste.

Divide the dough into 4, put on a lightly floured surface and roll out each piece to about 17 cm/7 inches in diameter. Brush with a little oil and spoon over the tomato sauce. Put the spinach on the bases, leaving a space in the middle for the egg. Put the mozzarella on top of the spinach, drizzle with a little more oil and season with salt and plenty of black pepper.

Carefully transfer to the hot pizza stone or baking sheet and cook for 10 minutes. Remove from the oven and crack an egg into the middle of each pizza. Top with the fontina or Gruyère and return to the oven for a further 5–10 minutes, until the base is crisp and golden and the eggs have just set. Serve immediately.

Sicilian prawn/shrimp and tomato pizza

½ recipe Sicilian Pizza Dough (page 14), making just 1 ball of dough

3–4 tablespoons Pizzaiola Sauce (page 18)

3 garlic cloves, sliced thinly

½ teaspoon red chilli flakes

10–12 medium uncooked prawns/shrimp, tail shells still attached

200 g/1 cup very ripe cherry tomatoes or any other very tasty small tomatoes

a good handful of fresh flat leaf parsley, roughly chopped

extra virgin olive oil, to drizzle

sea salt and freshly ground black pepper

lemon wedges, to serve

a testo, terracotta bakestone or a large, heavy baking sheet

a pizza peel or rimless baking sheet

Makes 1 medium-crust pizza, 25–35 cm/10–14 inches

Using the plumpest raw prawns/shrimp you can find will ensure that they don't toughen up through over-cooking. Avoid using pre-cooked prawns, which will make the end result dry, chewy and unappetizing. If you do have to use the pre-cooked variety, pop them onto the pizza 5 minutes from the end of cooking time.

Put the testo, terracotta bakestone or a large, heavy baking sheet on the lower shelf of the oven. Preheat the oven to 220°C (425°F) Gas 7 for at least 30 minutes.

Uncover the dough, punch out the air and roll or pull into a 25-cm/10-inch circle directly onto non-stick baking parchment. Slide this onto the pizza peel or rimless baking sheet. Spread the pizzaiola sauce over the pizza base, leaving a 1-cm/½-inch rim around the edge. Scatter with the garlic, chilli flakes, prawns/shrimp and tomatoes. Season.

Working quickly, open the oven door and slide paper and pizza onto the hot bakestone or baking sheet. If you are brave, try to shoot the pizza into the oven so that it leaves the paper behind – this takes practice!

Bake for 5 minutes, then carefully slide out the baking parchment. Bake the pizza for a further 15 minutes, or until the crust is golden and the prawns cooked. Remove from the oven, scatter with the parsley and drizzle with olive oil. Eat immediately with the lemon wedges for squeezing over the pizza.

pancetta pizza

For this recipe use very thinly sliced smoked pancetta (the Italian equivalent of streaky bacon, made from salt-cured pork belly). Pancetta comes in many forms: in whole cured slabs (with or without herbs and spices), smoked or unsmoked, or rolled up for slicing thinly, aged or not. The choice is endless and varies from region to region. Outside Italy, you can buy the smoked slab with rind, ready-sliced smoked or rolled unsmoked pancetta. Combined with Fiery Red Pesto, this is incredible!

1 recipe Basic Pizza Dough (page 13)

6 tablespoons Fiery Red Pesto (page 20)

24 thin slices pancetta or thin streaky bacon

extra virgin olive oil, to drizzle

sea salt and freshly ground black pepper

a testo, terracotta bakestone or a large, heavy baking sheet

a pizza peel or rimless baking sheet

Makes 1 medium-crust pizza, approximately 20 x 40 cm/ 8 x 16 inches

Put the testo, terracotta bakestone or a large, heavy baking sheet on the lower shelf of the oven. Preheat the oven to 220°C (425°F) Gas 7 for at least 30 minutes.

Uncover the dough, punch out the air and roll or pull into a rectangle, about 20 cm/8 inches wide and as long as your oven will take (you can always make 2 shorter ones). Roll the dough directly onto non-stick baking parchment. Slide this onto the pizza peel or rimless baking sheet.

Spread the red pesto over the pizza base, leaving a 1-cm/½-inch rim around the edge. Lay the strips of pancetta widthways across the pizza – they should be almost the same width as the dough. Season and drizzle with oil.

Working quickly, open the oven door and slide paper and pizza onto the hot bakestone or baking sheet. If you are brave, try to shoot the pizza into the oven so that it leaves the paper behind – this takes practice!

Bake for 5 minutes, then carefully slide out the baking parchment. Bake the pizza for a further 15 minutes, or until the crust is golden and the pancetta crisp. Remove from the oven and drizzle with olive oil. Cut into fingers and eat immediately.

½ recipe Basic Pizza Dough (page 13), making just 1 ball of dough

100 g/3½ oz. buffalo mozzarella or cow's milk mozzarella (*fior di latte*)

100 g/3½ oz. artichokes preserved in oil (or grilled artichokes from a deli)

1–2 garlic cloves, finely chopped

2 tablespoons extra virgin olive oil, plus extra to drizzle

6–8 juicy black olives

2 tablespoons roughly chopped fresh flat leaf parsley

sea salt and freshly ground black pepper

a testo, terracotta bakestone or a large, heavy baking sheet

a pizza peel or rimless baking sheet

Makes 1 medium-crust pizza, 25–35 cm/10–14 inches, or 2 small pizzas

Artichokes preserved in oil for antipasti are perfect for pizza-making as the delicious oil they are soaked in means they won't dry out during cooking. You can also make this with smoked mozzarella and it is equally delicious.

pizza with artichokes and mozzarella

Put the testo, terracotta bakestone or a large, heavy baking sheet on the lower shelf of the oven. Preheat the oven to 220°C (425°F) Gas 7 for at least 30 minutes.

Lightly squeeze any excess moisture out of the mozzarella, then slice it and leave the slices on kitchen paper for 5 minutes to absorb any remaining moisture. Cut the artichokes into quarters and toss them with the garlic and olive oil.

Uncover the dough, punch out the air and roll or pull into a 25-cm/10-inch circle directly onto non-stick baking parchment. Slide this onto the pizza peel or rimless baking sheet. Arrange the mozzarella evenly over the pizza base, leaving a 1-cm/½-inch rim around the edge. Scatter the artichoke and olives over the mozzarella, then season and drizzle with olive oil.

Working quickly, open the oven door and slide paper and pizza onto the hot bakestone or baking sheet. If you are brave, try to shoot the pizza into the oven so that it leaves the paper behind – this takes practice!

Bake for 5 minutes, then carefully slide out the baking parchment. Bake the pizza for a further 15 minutes, or until the crust is golden and the cheese melted and bubbling. Remove from the oven and sprinkle the parsley and freshly ground pepper over the top. Eat immediately.

pizza piccante

½ recipe Sicilian Pizza Dough (page 14), making just 1 ball of dough

4 tablespoons Pizzaiola Sauce (page 18)

50 g/2 oz. buffalo mozzarella or cow's milk mozzarella (*fior di latte*)

3 large garlic cloves, thinly sliced

50 g/2 oz. *provolone piccante*, thinly sliced

2 fat red chillies (or more), thinly sliced

extra virgin olive oil, to drizzle

chilli oil, to drizzle

sea salt and freshly crushed black pepper

a testo, terracotta bakestone or a large, heavy baking sheet

a pizza peel or rimless baking sheet

Makes 1 medium-crust pizza, 25–35 cm/10-14 inches

This contains all the heat of southern Italy. *Provolone piccante*, originally from Campania, is a sharp, aged cow's milk cheese often found in a globe shape and usually covered in a waxed rind. It makes a delicious sandwich with fresh tomato, dried oregano and a drizzle of olive oil.

Put the testo, terracotta bakestone or a large, heavy baking sheet on the lower shelf of the oven. Preheat the oven to 220°C (425°F) Gas 7 for at least 30 minutes.

Lightly squeeze any excess moisture out of the mozzarella, then slice it and leave the slices on kitchen paper for 5 minutes to absorb any remaining moisture.

Uncover the dough, punch out the air and roll or pull into a 25-cm/10-inch circle directly onto non-stick baking parchment. Slide this onto the pizza peel or rimless baking sheet. Spread the pizzaiola sauce over the pizza base, leaving a 1-cm½-inch rim around the edge. Scatter the garlic over the top. Arrange the provolone and mozzarella on top and scatter with the chillies. Season well with plenty of crushed black pepper and drizzle with olive oil.

Working quickly, open the oven door and slide paper and pizza onto the hot bakestone or baking sheet. If you are brave, try to shoot the pizza into the oven so that it leaves the paper behind – this takes practice!

Bake for 5 minutes, then carefully slide out the baking parchment. Bake the pizza for a further 15 minutes, or until the crust is golden and the cheese melted and bubbling. Remove from the oven and drizzle with the chilli oil. Eat immediately.

pear, pecorino and Taleggio pizza with honey and sage

½ recipe Basic Pizza Dough (page 13), making just 1 ball of dough

2 tablespoons extra virgin olive oil, plus extra to drizzle

125 g/4 oz. Taleggio (rind removed), cubed

1 very ripe pear, cored and thinly sliced

12–15 small sage leaves

50 g/½ cup freshly grated pecorino cheese

1 tablespoon runny honey (acacia or orange blossom, if possible)

sea salt and freshly ground black pepper

a testo, terracotta bakestone or a large, heavy baking sheet

a pizza peel or rimless baking sheet

Makes 1 medium-crust pizza, 25–35 cm/10–14 inches

This is a sort of new-wave pizza, and very popular in Italian city pizzerias. Soft, buttery Taleggio, made in the valleys and mountains of Lombardy and the Valtellina, melts and runs very quickly, so make sure it's not near the edge of the pizza. Ripe, juicy pear is the perfect foil for this cheese, and don't leave out the sage – it's integral to the flavour.

Put the testo, terracotta bakestone or a large, heavy baking sheet on the lower shelf of the oven. Preheat the oven to 220°C (425°F) Gas 7 for at least 30 minutes.

Uncover the dough, punch out the air and roll or pull into a 25-cm/10-inch circle directly onto non-stick baking parchment. Slide this onto the pizza peel or rimless baking sheet. Rub the pizza base with the olive oil and scatter over the Taleggio. Arrange the pears over this, then the sage and pecorino. Drizzle with the honey, then season and drizzle with a little more olive oil.

Working quickly, open the oven door and slide paper and pizza onto the hot bakestone or baking sheet. If you are brave, try to shoot the pizza into the oven so that it leaves the paper behind – this takes practice!

Bake for 5 minutes, then carefully slide out the baking parchment. Bake the pizza for a further 15 minutes, or until the crust is golden and the cheese melted and bubbling. Sprinkle with freshly ground black pepper and eat immediately.

pizzas, thick and thin 49

potato and radicchio pizza

15 g/½ oz. fresh/compressed yeast, 1 tablespoon dried active baking yeast, or 1 sachet/package fast-action/quick-rising yeast

a pinch of sugar

250 ml/1 cup warm water

350 g/2⅓ cups plain white/all-purpose flour, plus extra for dusting

1 tablespoon olive oil

a pinch of salt

Potato topping

1 medium potato, peeled and sliced extremely thinly

150 g/6 oz. Fontina, Taleggio or mozzarella cheese

1 large radicchio, cut into about 8 wedges, brushed with olive oil and grilled/broiled for 5 minutes

1 tablespoon chopped fresh thyme

sea salt and freshly ground black pepper

extra olive oil, for trickling

a baking pan, about 23 x 33 cm/ 11 x 13 inches

Serves 2–4, depending on appetite

In general, Italians like to stick to the classics when it comes to pizza, but with a little imagination, pizza toppings are limitless. This combination of thinly sliced potato, cheese, bitter radicchio and fresh thyme is sublime.

To make the dough, put the fresh yeast and sugar in a medium bowl and beat until creamy. Whisk in the warm water and leave for 10 minutes until frothy. For other yeasts, use according to the packet instructions.

Sift the flour into a large bowl and make a hollow in the centre. Pour in the yeast mixture, olive oil and a good pinch of salt. Mix with a round-bladed knife, then your hands, until the dough comes together. Transfer to a floured surface, wash and dry your hands and knead for 10 minutes until smooth and elastic. The dough should be quite soft, but if too soft to handle, add more flour, 1 tablespoon at a time. Put the dough in a clean, oiled bowl, cover with a damp tea towel or clingfilm/plastic wrap and let rise until doubled in size – about 1 hour.

When risen, punch down the dough with your fists, then roll out or pat into a rectangle that will fit in the baking pan, pushing it up the sides a little. Cover the top with a thin layer of sliced potato, then half the cheese, the wedges of radicchio, then the remaining cheese. Season with salt and pepper, and sprinkle with thyme.

Trickle oil over the top and let rise in a warm place for 10 minutes. Bake in a preheated oven at 220°C (425°F) Gas 7 for 15–20 minutes or until golden and bubbling.

You will see mounds of this thick pizza, or *sfinciune* as it is known locally, on food stalls all over Palermo. It is the ultimate snack on the run and is perfect for picnics and lunchboxes. It may seem strange, but in Sicily, breadcrumbs are sprinkled over pasta and even on top of pizza. Make sure you use good olive oil here.

Palermo pizza

2 recipes Sicilian Pizza Dough (page 14), making the changes stated in this recipe

7 tablespoons olive oil, plus extra to drizzle

1 large onion, sliced

3 large, ripe tomatoes, chopped

1 teaspoon dried oregano, plus extra to taste

8 anchovy fillets in oil, drained and chopped

75 g/1 cup dried breadcrumbs

75 g/2½ cups caciocavallo (or Emmental) cheese, cubed

sea salt and freshly ground black pepper

a rectangular baking pan, 35 x 25 x 3 cm/ 14 x 10 x 1¼ inches, oiled

a testo, terracotta bakestone or a large, heavy baking sheet

Makes 1 thick pizza, 35 x 25 cm/14 x 10 inches

When you make the pizza dough, replace the lemon juice with olive oil. Rise once, then punch down the air, knead lightly and roll or pull into a rectangle that will fit into the prepared baking pan. Cover the pan lightly with clingfilm/plastic wrap or a damp tea towel and leave in a warm place to rise until it has reached the top of the pan (about 30 minutes).

While the dough is rising, put the testo, terracotta bakestone or a large, heavy baking sheet on the lower shelf of the oven. Preheat the oven to 220°C (425°F) Gas 7 for at least 30 minutes.

To make the sauce, heat 4 tablespoons of the olive oil in a saucepan and add the onion. Cook until soft but not coloured, then add the tomatoes, dried oregano and anchovy fillets. Cook for 5 minutes until the anchovies dissolve and the tomatoes collapse. Season to taste.

Heat the remaining olive oil in a frying pan and fry the breadcrumbs until golden and crisp.

When the dough has risen, uncover and dimple the top lightly with your fingers as if you were making focaccia, but don't make too many holes. Spread with half of the sauce and bake for 25 minutes.

Remove from the oven, spread the remaining sauce over the top, scatter over the breadcrumbs and extra oregano and drizzle with olive oil. Finish by scattering the caciocavallo over everything, then bake for another 5 minutes until the top is golden. Serve warm or cold, cut into squares.

750 g/1¾ lb. floury-fleshed potatoes (King Edwards, Golden Wonder, Red Rooster), unpeeled

2 tablespoons olive oil, plus extra to drizzle

6–8 cherry or baby plum tomatoes, halved

50 g/½ cup black wrinkly olives, pits in

25 g salted capers, rinsed

3 salted anchovies, rinsed

1 small red onion, sliced into thin rings and tossed in olive oil

1 teaspoon dried oregano

sea salt and freshly ground black pepper

a shallow sandwich pan or pizza pan, 23 cm/9 inches, oiled

Makes 1 pizza, 23 cm/9 inches

potato-based pizza

Although not crispy like a pizza, this is a wonderful alternative for those who love mashed potato or who are wheat intolerant, and it is popular in southern Italian homes. If you are not keen on anchovies, try using tinned tuna – you can really try any pizza topping you like, even mozzarella. Have some pizzaiola sauce to serve on the side, along with barbecued sausages for any meat-eaters. Other recipes for potato pizza incorporate mashed potato in normal pizza dough, which is delicious, but a little heavy, and obviously not wheat-free.

Preheat the oven to 200°C (400°F) Gas 6.

Boil the potatoes in plenty of salted water until tender. Drain well and carefully peel off the skins. Mash the potatoes or push them through a potato ricer, then leave to cool for 5 minutes. Beat in the olive oil and season to taste. Spoon into the prepared sandwich pan or pizza pan and smooth out the surface.

Top with the tomatoes, olives, capers, anchovies and onion rings. Sprinkle with the dried oregano and drizzle with olive oil. Bake in the oven for 20 minutes until sizzling. Serve hot or cold.

wheat-free pizza with roasted vegetables

This wheat-free pizza is very good, but don't expect a pizza-like dough. It starts life as a batter and when baked, becomes chewy and sponge-like on the inside, with a crisp crust. The recipe uses a gluten-free flour and is perfect for those who can't eat wheat but still crave that unique pizza experience.

½ aubergine/eggplant, cubed

1 small red pepper, deseeded and cut into strips

1 small courgette/zucchini, sliced

2 garlic cloves, sliced

6 tablespoons olive oil, plus extra to drizzle

3 tablespoons each milk and water, mixed together and warmed

¾ teaspoon freshly squeezed lemon juice

1 egg

½ teaspoon salt

225 g/1¾ cups gluten-free white bread flour, such as Dove's Farm or Bob's Red Mill

1 teaspoon fast-action/quick-rising dried yeast

75 g/2½ oz. mozzarella, drained and cubed (optional)

sea salt and freshly ground black pepper

a shallow pizza pan, 23 cm/ 9 inches, oiled

Makes 1 pizza, 23 cm/9 inches

Preheat the oven to 200°C (400°F) Gas 6.

Toss the aubergine/eggplant, red pepper, courgette/zucchini and garlic in 4 tablespoons of the olive oil and roast on a roasting tray in the oven for 15–20 minutes, or until they are beginning to soften.

While the vegetables are roasting, make the batter. Whisk the warm (not hot) milk and water, the lemon juice, remaining olive oil, egg and salt together. Beat in the flour and yeast and mix until well combined. Pour into the prepared pizza pan, cover and leave to rise in a warm place for about 20 minutes or until puffy.

Bake the pizza base in the oven for 10 minutes to set the dough, then quickly remove from the oven and scatter with the roasted vegetables and mozzarella (if using). Season well, drizzle with olive oil and return to the oven for a further 10 minutes until the vegetables are sizzling and the pizza has slightly shrunk from the edges. Cut into wedges and serve hot.

pizza pockets

½ recipe Basic Pizza Dough (page 13), making just 1 ball of dough

a testo, terracotta bakestone or a large, heavy baking sheet

Makes 4–6 pizza pockets, depending on size

Do try these – they are very easy to make, versatile, and the result is so professional. Indeed, they are becoming a very popular snack. Once baked, they can be frozen and reheated, as long as they are wrapped in aluminium foil to keep them moist. They must be warm when they are split or they will crack.

Place the testo, terracotta bakestone or a large heavy baking sheet on the lower shelf of the oven. Preheat the oven to 220°C (425°F) Gas 7 for at least 30 minutes.

Uncover the dough, punch out the air and divide it into 6 (or however many you wish). Shape each piece into a round ball then roll out to an oval. Using a fork with large tines, prick them all over (but not too much).

Lay the pizza pockets on 2 sheets of lightly floured baking parchment. If they don't all fit, bake them in batches.

Working quickly, open the oven door and slide the paper onto the hot bakestone or baking sheet.

Bake for 3–5 minutes, until very puffed up and very pale golden. Remove from the oven and wrap in a clean tea towel to keep warm and soft if you need to cook another batch.

When they are all cooked, quickly cut them in half across the middle and open out the pocket. Stuff with your chosen filling, for example cooked ham, tomato and mozzarella. Wrap loosely in aluminium foil, then return to the oven for 2 minutes. Unwrap, add salad leaves and eat immediately.

Schiacciata is a dialect word meaning 'flattened', so pizza is sometimes known as schiacciata, i.e. a flattened bread dough. If, after making pizza, you find you have some dough left over (and some good olives to hand) this is the recipe for you. There is no olive oil needed here, but you can have some really good oil in a little pot ready for dipping the hot pizzas into.

crispy olive schiacciate

any leftover Basic Pizza Dough (page 13)

a splash of white wine

a handful of green olives, pitted and roughly chopped

rock salt

extra virgin olive oil or Black Olive and Tomato Relish (page 20), to serve

a testo, terracotta bakestone or a large, heavy baking sheet

a large rimless baking sheet

Put the testo, terracotta bakestone or a large, heavy baking sheet on the lower shelf of the oven. Preheat the oven to 220°C (425°F) Gas 7 for at least 30 minutes.

Using a rolling pin, roll the dough out as thinly as you can, directly onto the baking sheet. Brush the dough with a little white wine, scatter with the olives and sprinkle with rock salt. Lightly press the olives and salt into the dough. Using a pizza wheel, score the dough in lozenge shapes directly on the baking sheet.

Bake for 5–10 minutes until the schiacciate are puffed and pale golden. Remove from the oven and break up into the pre-cut lozenges. Serve warm with olive oil or Black Olive and Tomato Relish.

Calzone is a close cousin to pizza – the delicious hot fillings are encased in folded dough rather than arranged sitting on top. Equally indulgent are deep filled pizza pies, often rustic in style, and always rich and filling.

calzones and pizza pies

This is a good calzone to make for more than two people. The vegetables can be chopped as roughly as you like, but the aubergine/eggplant must be cooked through before it goes into the dough. You can add a little pizzaiola sauce to make it more tomatoey.

calzone alla parmigiana

1 recipe Basic Pizza Dough (page 13), up to the first rising

2 aubergines/eggplants, cubed

12 whole garlic cloves, peeled

4 tablespoons extra virgin olive oil, plus extra to glaze

200 g/6½ oz. buffalo mozzarella or cow's milk mozzarella (*fior di latte*)

5 ripe tomatoes, cubed

3 tablespoons chopped fresh basil

4 tablespoons freshly grated Parmesan cheese

sea salt and freshly ground black pepper

2 large, heavy baking sheets

2 rimless baking sheets

Makes 4 calzone

Put the baking sheets into the oven. Preheat the oven to 200°C (400°F) Gas 6 for at least 30 minutes.

Uncover the dough, punch out the air and divide into 4 balls. Dredge with flour and leave to rise on floured baking parchment for about 20 minutes, until soft and puffy.

Meanwhile, toss the aubergine/eggplant and garlic cloves with the olive oil in a roasting pan and roast for 20 minutes.

Lightly squeeze any excess moisture out of the mozzarella then cut it into cubes. Remove the roasting pan from the oven and cool for 10 minutes before stirring in the tomatoes, mozzarella and basil. Season to taste.

Roll or pull the risen balls of dough into 20-cm/8-inch circles directly onto 2 sheets of non-stick baking parchment. Slide these onto 2 rimless baking sheets. Spread a quarter of the vegetable mixture on one half of each calzone, leaving just over 1 cm/½ inch around the edge. Season well. Fold the uncovered half of the dough over the filling. Pinch and twist the edges firmly together so that the filling doesn't escape during cooking. Brush with olive oil and sprinkle with Parmesan.

Working quickly, open the oven door and slide paper and calzone onto the hot baking sheets. Bake for 30 minutes, swapping the baking sheets around halfway or until the crust is puffed up and golden. Remove from the oven and leave to stand for 2–3 minutes before serving (this will allow the filling to cool slightly). Serve hot or warm.

½ recipe Basic Pizza Dough (page 13), making just 1 ball of dough

50–75 g/2–3 oz. buffalo mozzarella or cow's milk mozzarella (*fior di latte*)

200 g/7 oz. potatoes, peeled and very thinly sliced

2 tablespoons extra virgin olive oil, plus extra to glaze

1 garlic clove, finely chopped

1 tablespoon chopped fresh rosemary

sea salt and freshly ground black pepper

a testo, terracotta bakestone or a large, heavy baking sheet

a pizza peel or rimless baking sheet

Makes 1 calzone, 25–35 cm/ 10–14 inches

potato and mozzarella calzone

In Naples, this is known as 'filled pizza' or *pizza ripieno*, but the word *calzone* literally means 'trouser leg' as it was thought the shape was reminiscent of the traditional everyday dress of the street – a sort of tapered pantaloon.

Put the testo, terracotta bakestone or a large, heavy baking sheet on the lower shelf of the oven. Preheat the oven to 220°C (425°F) Gas 7 for at least 30 minutes.

Lightly squeeze any excess moisture out of the mozzarella then cut it into cubes. Toss the sliced potato with the olive oil, garlic and rosemary, then add the mozzarella.

Uncover the dough, punch out the air and roll or pull into a 25-cm/10-inch circle directly onto non-stick baking parchment. Slide this onto the pizza peel or rimless baking sheet. Spread one half of the calzone with the potato mixture, leaving just over 1 cm/½ inch around the edge. Season well. Fold the uncovered half of the dough over the filling. Pinch and twist the edges firmly together so that the filling doesn't escape during cooking.

Working quickly, open the oven door and slide paper and calzone onto the hot bakestone or baking sheet. If you are brave, try to shoot it into the oven so that it leaves the paper behind – this takes practice!

Bake for 10 minutes, then carefully slide out the baking parchment. Bake for a further 25–30 minutes or until the crust is puffed up and golden. Remove from the oven and brush with a little olive oil. Leave to stand for 2–3 minutes before serving (this will allow the filling to cool slightly). Serve hot or warm.

egg and spinach pizza pies

1 recipe Basic Pizza Dough
(page 13) or Sicilian Pizza Dough
(page 14)

2 tablespoons extra virgin olive oil,
plus extra to glaze

1 small onion, finely chopped

250 g/8 oz. fresh spinach, washed

250 g/8 oz. ricotta

4 tablespoons freshly grated
Parmesan cheese

75 g/2¼ cups rocket/arugula,
finely chopped

1 teaspoon chopped fresh
tarragon

freshly grated nutmeg

8 eggs

sea salt and freshly ground
black pepper

*a testo, terracotta bakestone
or a large, heavy baking sheet*

two 4-hole muffin pans

Makes 8 pizza pies

These little pies could be made into a traditional calzone by breaking a whole egg into the filling, but for a special occasion or a picnic, they look great cooked in muffin pans.

Place the testo, terracotta bakestone or a large, heavy baking sheet on the lower shelf of the oven. Preheat the oven to 220°C (425°F) Gas 7 for at least 30 minutes.

Heat the olive oil in a frying pan, add the onion and fry for 5 minutes until golden. Leave to cool. Steam the spinach until just wilted, refresh in cold water, then squeeze out as much moisture as possible and roughly chop. Beat the spinach and onions into the ricotta with the Parmesan, rocket and tarragon. Season well with salt, pepper and nutmeg.

Uncover the dough, punch out the air then tip out onto a floured surface. Roll or pull to a thin disc. Cut out 8 circles roughly 16 cm/6 inches in diameter. Use these to line each muffin cup. Fill each pie with some of the ricotta mixture. Make a small indent in each filling. Break the eggs one at a time, separating the yolks from the whites. Slip a yolk into the indent of each pie. Season. Roll the dough offcuts into long, thin ropes and cut into 16 lengths. Use these to make a cross on top of each pie, sealing the edges with a little water. Brush lightly with olive oil.

Bake in the oven for 10 minutes until the egg is just set and the dough cooked. Eat hot.

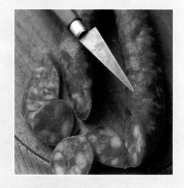

At one time, this rustic country pie was made with sweet pastry but nowadays it is made with pizza dough. You can use any filling you like, but ricotta and pockets of melting mozzarella are essential. It is very rich and filling, and equally good eaten at room temperature.

torta rustica

1 recipe Basic Pizza Dough (page 13)

5 eggs, separated

300 g/10 oz. ricotta, sieved

100 g/3½ oz. cow's milk mozzarella (*fior di latte*), diced

100 g/3½ oz. smoked mozzarella, diced

55 g/2 oz. Speck ham, chopped

55 g/2 oz. salami, chopped

4 tablespoons freshly grated Parmesan cheese

10 cherry tomatoes, halved

sea salt and freshly ground black pepper

a pizza pan or springform cake pan, 25 x 4 cm/10 x 1¾ inches, lightly oiled

Makes 1 pie, 25 cm/10 inches

Place a baking sheet in the middle of the oven. Preheat the oven to 180°C (350°F) Gas 4.

Beat 4 of the egg yolks together, then beat into the ricotta with plenty of salt and pepper. Whisk all the egg whites until stiff and fold into the ricotta mixture. Now fold in both types of mozzarella, the Speck and salami, and finally the Parmesan.

Uncover the dough, punch out the air and roll or pull two-thirds of it into a 35-cm/14-inch circle. Use this to line the pizza pan, draping the extra dough over the edge. Spoon in the filling and smooth out the surface. Roll out the remaining dough thinly on a floured surface. Cut it into narrow strips and use them to make a lattice over the top of the pie. Secure the ends to the edge of the pastry with a little water. Trim around the edge with a sharp knife. Place a halved cherry tomato in each square of the lattice and season again. Beat the remaining egg yolk with a pinch of salt and brush the edges of the pie with it.

Bake in the oven for 40–45 minutes until golden. Remove from the oven and leave to stand for 10 minutes before serving.

stromboli

1 recipe Basic Pizza Dough
(page 13) or Sicilian Pizza Dough
(page 14)

8 tablespoons Fiery Red Pesto
(page 20)

4 large red peppers

4 tablespoons olive oil

125 g/4 oz. black olives,
pitted and chopped

*a large baking sheet, lined
with parchment paper*

Makes 4 stromboli

These little filled and rolled pizzas are called *stromboli*. Stromboli is a live volcano and one of the Aeolian islands off the coast of northern Sicily. Maybe it describes the eruption of flavours and filling when the pizzas are cut open, or the black and red colours of the filling. These are better eaten at room temperature and are perfect for picnics and packed lunches. Meat-eaters can cover the red pepper with slices of cooked ham before rolling up.

Preheat the oven to 200°C (400°F) Gas 6.

Rub the peppers with the olive oil and roast in the oven for 25–30 minutes until charred on the outside. Peel the peppers, pull them apart and remove the seeds and stalks. Leave to cool.

Meanwhile, uncover the dough, punch out the air and knead half the olives into it. Divide the dough into 4. Roll each piece into a rectangle about 17 x 24 cm/7 x 10 inches. Spread pesto over each one, sprinkle the remaining chopped olives over the top, and cover with the peppers, leaving a 1-cm/½-inch rim around the edges of the dough. Roll up from the shorter side. Make sure the seam is underneath the pizza. Pinch the open ends to seal, and tuck them under. Squash the rolled pizzas slightly – they should now look a little like French pains au chocolat. Arrange them well apart on the prepared baking sheet, cover with lightly oiled clingfilm/plastic wrap and leave to rise for 20 minutes.

Remove the clingfilm and bake the stromboli for 25–30 minutes until risen and golden. Leave to cool for 5 minutes before cutting open and serving, or leave to cool completely.

15 g/½ cake fresh/compressed yeast, 1 tablespoon dried active baking yeast, or 1 sachet/package fast-action/quick-rising yeast

a pinch of sugar

250 ml/1 cup warm water

350 g/2⅓ cups plain white/all-purpose flour, plus extra to dust

1 tablespoon olive oil, plus extra for brushing

a pinch of salt

Filling

100 g/3½ oz. cubed melting cheese, such as mozzarella

100 g/3½ oz. cubed salami, ham or cooked sausage

50 g/⅓ cup cooked chopped spinach

4 sun-dried tomatoes in oil, chopped

3–4 tablespoons tomato sauce, Salsa Pizzaiola (page 18) or similar

2–3 tablespoons chopped mixed herbs

sea salt and freshly ground black pepper

a floured baking sheet

Makes 2

Italians are very thrifty, and a really delicious double-crust pizza can be made with a carefully chosen mixture of leftovers. There must be cheese or béchamel sauce to keep it moist, but you can add anchovies, cooked meat sauce, capers, olives – whatever you like, as long as their flavours suit each other.

pizza rustica

To make the dough, put the fresh yeast and sugar in a medium bowl and beat until creamy. Whisk in the warm water and leave for 10 minutes until frothy. For other yeasts, use according to the packet instructions.

Sift the flour into a large bowl and make a hollow in the centre. Pour in the yeast mixture, olive oil and a good pinch of salt. Mix with a round-bladed knife, then your hands, until the dough comes together. Transfer to a floured surface, wash and dry your hands and knead for 10 minutes until smooth and elastic. The dough should be quite soft, but if too soft to handle, add more flour, 1 tablespoon at a time. Put the dough in a clean, oiled bowl, cover with a damp tea towel or clingfilm/plastic wrap and let rise until doubled in size – about 1 hour.

To make the filling, put the mozzarella, salami, spinach, sun-dried tomatoes, tomato sauce and mixed herbs in a bowl and season with salt and pepper.

Roll out the dough to a large circle, making sure it is well floured so it doesn't stick. Pile the filling onto one half of the dough, avoiding the edges. Flip over the other half to cover, press the edges together to seal, then twist and crimp. Slide onto a floured baking sheet and brush lightly with olive oil. Make a slash in the top or it could explode when cooking.

Bake in a preheated oven at 220°C (425°F) Gas 7 for about 25 minutes until golden and firm. Remove from the oven, set aside for 5 minutes, then serve.

This magnificent double-crust pie is filled with Sicilian bounty – aubergines/eggplants, tomatoes, tuna and basil. The breadcrumbs between the layers soak up the juices and keep the filling firm but moist. Tinned tuna in oil works very well and if you are feeling brave, you can even make this with fresh, boned sardines instead of tuna.

aubergine/eggplant and tuna double-crust pizza

1 recipe Sicilian Pizza Dough (page 14)

4 tablespoons Classic Pesto Genovese (page 20)

4 tablespoons extra virgin olive oil, plus extra to glaze

2 aubergines/eggplants, thinly sliced

55 g/½ cup dried breadcrumbs

55 g/½ cup freshly grated pecorino cheese

two 150-g/5-oz. fresh tuna steaks, sliced horizontally

4 tomatoes, thinly sliced

sea salt and freshly ground black pepper

a testo, terracotta bakestone or a large, heavy baking sheet

a pizza pan or springform cake pan, 25 x 4 cm, 10 x 1¾ inches, lightly oiled

Makes 1 pie, 25 cm/10 inches

Put the testo, terracotta bakestone or a large, heavy baking sheet on the lower shelf of the oven. Preheat the oven to 220°C (425°F) Gas 7 for at least 30 minutes.

Heat the olive oil in a frying pan and fry the aubergines/eggplants until golden brown. Drain on kitchen paper. Mix the breadcrumbs with the pecorino.

Uncover the dough, punch out the air and roll or pull two-thirds of it into a 35-cm/14-inch circle. Use this to line the pizza pan, draping the extra dough over the edge. Arrange the aubergine slices over the base and sprinkle with a quarter of the breadcrumb mixture. Arrange the tuna slices on top and spread over the pesto. Sprinkle with another quarter of the breadcrumb mixture. Arrange the tomatoes over the tuna and pesto, season and sprinkle with another quarter of the breadcrumb mixture.

Roll or pull the remaining dough into a 27-cm/11-inch circle. Brush the edge of the dough with a little water. Lay the circle of dough over the pie and press the edges to seal. Trim off the excess dough with a sharp knife. Brush the top with olive oil and sprinkle with the remaining breadcrumb mixture. Make 2 slashes in the centre of the pie. Bake in the oven for 35–45 minutes until golden. Serve warm or cold.

Italian sausage, potato and ricotta double-crust pizza

This delicious double-crust pizza was made famous by the nuns of San Vito lo Capo in Sicily.

1 recipe Sicilian Pizza Dough (page 14)

2 tablespoons extra virgin olive oil, plus extra to glaze

200 g/7 oz. potatoes, peeled and finely diced

2 onions, finely chopped

1 teaspoon dried oregano

250 g/8 oz. fresh Italian sausage, skinned

1 teaspoon fennel seeds

2 tablespoons chopped fresh sage

125 g/4 oz. ricotta

sea salt and freshly ground black pepper

a testo, terracotta bakestone or a large, heavy baking sheet

a rimless baking sheet

Makes 1 double-crust pizza, 30 cm/12 inches

Place the testo, terracotta bakestone or a large, heavy baking sheet on the lower shelf of the oven. Preheat the oven to 220°C (425°F) Gas 7 for at least 30 minutes.

Heat the oil in a frying pan and add the potatoes and onions. Cook for 5–10 minutes until the onion starts to colour and the potato is soft. Stir in the oregano. Season, then transfer to a bowl to cool. Fry the sausage briefly in the same frying pan, breaking it up with the back of a fork. Add the fennel seeds and sage and fry for a couple of minutes – but not too long or the meat will toughen. Season well, then leave to cool.

Uncover the dough, knock out the air and divide into 2. Roll each piece into a thin, 30-cm/12-inch circle directly onto baking parchment. Spread the potato and onion mixture onto one circle, leaving a 1-cm/½-inch rim around the edge. Dot with the sausage and the cheese. Season. Brush the edge with water and lay the remaining circle on top. Pinch and roll the edges to seal. Brush with a little olive oil. Make 2 slashes in the centre of the pie, then slide onto the rimless baking sheet. Working quickly, open the oven door and slide paper and pizza onto the hot bakestone or baking sheet. If you are brave, try to shoot the pizza into the oven so that it leaves the paper behind – this takes practice!

Bake for 10 minutes, then carefully slide out the baking parchment. Bake the pizza for a further 25–30 minutes, or until the crust is puffed up and golden. Remove from the oven and brush with a little olive oil. Leave to stand for 5 minutes before serving. Eat hot, warm or cold.

1 recipe Classic Pesto Genovese (page 20)

500 g/4¼ cups Italian '00' flour or plain white/all-purpose flour

1 teaspoon sugar

½ teaspoon fine sea salt

25 g/1 cake fresh/compressed yeast, 1 tablespoon dried active yeast or 2 teaspoons fast-action/quick-rising dried yeast

1 egg, beaten

3 tablespoons extra virgin olive oil

350 ml/1⅔ cups hand-hot water

200 g/7 oz. large green olives, stoned and roughly chopped

200 g/3 cups freshly grated pecorino or Parmesan cheese

2–3 tablespoons garlic-infused olive oil

sea salt and freshly ground black pepper

a pizza peel or rimless baking sheet

a terracotta bakestone or a large, heavy baking sheet

Serves 6 as a loaf

rolled pesto, olive and garlic bread

This is almost an Italian equivalent of hot garlic bread, but much better. You can use ordinary pizza dough, or enrich it with egg. The thin dough base is smothered in pesto and green olives, rolled up to look like a long Swiss/jelly roll and left to rise again. Drenched in garlic oil and smothered in pecorino, the smell alone wafting from the oven is to die for!

Sift the flour, sugar and salt into a large bowl and make a well in the centre. Crumble in the fresh/compressed yeast or sprinkle in the dried yeast, if using. If you are using dried active yeast, follow the manufacturer's instructions. Rub in the yeast until the mixture resembles fine breadcrumbs. Pour in the beaten egg, olive oil and the hand-hot water and mix until the dough comes together. Knead the dough energetically, on a floured surface, for 5 minutes until soft, smooth and elastic. Put it in a lightly oiled bowl, cover with clingfilm/plastic wrap or a damp tea towel and leave to rise in a warm place until doubled in size – about 1½ hours. Preheat the oven to 200°C (400°F) Gas 6.

When risen, knock back the dough, then roll or pull into a large rectangle as thinly as you can, directly onto a sheet of non-stick baking parchment. Spread the dough liberally with the pesto, leaving a 1-cm/½-inch rim all around the dough, then scatter over the olives and 125 g/1¾ cups of the pecorino or Parmesan. Season. Using the parchment paper, roll the dough up like a Swiss/jelly roll, starting from the long side. Slide the dough onto another sheet of parchment making sure the seam is underneath. Brush with the garlic oil and sprinkle with the remaining cheese.

Slide the rolled bread onto the pizza peel or rimless baking sheet. Working quickly, open the oven door and slide paper and bread onto the hot bakestone or baking sheet. Bake for 20 minutes, then carefully slide out the baking parchment. Bake for a further 5 minutes until the crust is golden and the cheese melted but still white. Remove from the oven and serve warm (not hot) or cold in slices.

Focaccia literally means 'a bread that was baked on the hearth', but it is easy
to make in conventional ovens. It is found in many different forms in Italy
and can be thin and crisp, thick and soft, round or square.

focaccia

thin focaccia

1 recipe Basic Focaccia
(page 16), risen twice but
uncooked

100 ml/⅓ cup extra virgin olive oil

coarse sea salt or rock salt

*2 testi, terracotta bakestones
or large, heavy baking sheets*

*a rimless baking sheet,
lined with parchment paper*

Makes 2 large, flat focaccias

This is a wonderful example of the traditional focaccia, as it is baked directly on the bakestone or on a hot baking sheet. If the base is floured very well the focaccia can be slipped directly onto the stone or baking sheet, leaving the parchment paper behind. This is the kind of focaccia that you tear and dip into yet more fruity olive oil.

Put the 2 testi, terracotta bakestones or large, heavy baking sheets on the lower shelf of the oven. Preheat the oven to 220°C (425°F) Gas 7 for at least 30 minutes.

Uncover the dough, punch out the air and divide into 2. Shape each piece into a rough ball then pull and stretch the dough to a large oval shape – as large as will fit in your oven. Place on the rimless baking sheet. Cover with lightly oiled clingfilm/plastic wrap or a damp tea towel and leave to rise for 30 minutes.

Remove the clingfilm and, using your fingertips, make deep dimples all over the surface of the dough right down to the baking sheet. Drizzle over all but 2 tablespoons of the remaining oil. Spray the focaccias with water and sprinkle generously with salt. Working quickly, open the oven door and slide paper and focaccia onto the hot bakestones or baking sheet.

Bake for 15 minutes, then carefully slide out the baking parchment. Bake the focaccia for a further 15 minutes, or until the crust is golden. Brush or drizzle with the remaining olive oil then transfer to a wire rack to cool. Eat on the same day or leave to cool, then wrap up and freeze. When you remove it from the freezer, thaw and wrap in aluminium foil, then reheat for 5 minutes in a hot oven.

fennel and tomato focaccia

1 recipe Basic Focaccia
(page 16)

2 baby fennel bulbs, thinly sliced
and fronds chopped

2 tomatoes, thinly sliced

1½ teaspoons sea salt flakes

extra virgin olive oil, to serve

Serves 6-8

Fennel is widely eaten in Italy, and often served in a salad – finely shaved and simply dressed with olive oil, lemon juice and black pepper. Here its' aniseedy flavour is enhanced with roasting and, along with the tomatoes, makes a substantial topping for a simple focaccia dough.

Preheat the oven to 220°C (425°F) Gas 7. Uncover the risen dough and put it on a lightly oiled baking sheet. Using a lightly floured rolling pin, gently roll from the centre upwards in one motion, not pressing too firmly so that any air bubbles stay intact. Roll from the centre down to the opposite end to form a rough oval shape, about 30 cm/12 inches long and 20 cm/8 inches at its widest point. Lightly cover and let sit again for 20–30 minutes until it has risen.

Use the tips of your fingers to press dimples over the surface of the dough. Lay the fennel and tomato slices on top and scatter with the fronds. Drizzle with the remaining olive oil and sprinkle with the salt flakes. Bake in the preheated oven for 25 minutes. Carefully slide the focaccia off of the baking sheet and put it directly on the oven shelf. Cook for a further 5 minutes, until the crust is golden. Remove from the oven and let cool before eating. Serve with a small bowl of extra virgin olive oil for dipping.

sardenaira

This amazingly savoury Ligurian focaccia is topped with salted anchovies or salted sardines (hence the name). It is perfect for outdoor eating, served in thin slices with a cold glass of wine or beer.

25 g/1 cake fresh/compressed yeast, 1 tablespoon dried active baking yeast or 2 teaspoons fast-action/quick-rising dried yeast

½ teaspoon sugar

150 ml/⅔ cup warm milk

500 g/4¼ cups Italian '00' flour

7 tablespoons extra virgin olive oil

6 tablespoons hand-hot water

2 onions, thinly sliced

1 kg/2¼ lb. fresh, very ripe tomatoes, peeled and chopped, or 1 kg/2¼ lb. (drained weight) canned whole tomatoes

100 g/3½ oz. anchovies or sardines in salt

12 or more whole garlic cloves, unpeeled

100 g/3½ oz. or more small stoned black Ligurian olives

1 tablespoon dried oregano

sea salt and freshly ground black pepper

a rectangular baking pan, 28 x 43 cm/11 x 15 inches and approximately 2.5 cm/1 inch deep, oiled

Serves 10

In a large bowl, cream the fresh yeast with the sugar and whisk in the warm milk. Leave for 10 minutes until frothy. For other yeasts, follow the manufacturer's instructions.

Sift the flour with 1 teaspoon salt into a large bowl and make a well in the centre. Pour in the yeast mixture, 4 tablespoons of the olive oil and the hand-hot water. Mix together with a round-bladed knife, then use your hands until the dough comes together. Tip out onto a lightly floured surface, wash and dry your hands, then knead briskly for 10–15 minutes until smooth, shiny and elastic. Try not to add any extra flour at this stage – a wetter dough is better. If necessary, flour your hands and not the dough. If it is really too soft to handle, knead in a little more flour.

To test if the dough is ready, roll it into a fat sausage, take each end in either hand, lift the dough up and pull and stretch it outwards, gently wiggling it up and down – it should stretch out quite easily. If it doesn't, it needs more kneading. Shape into a neat ball. Put it in an oiled bowl, cover with clingfilm/plastic wrap or a damp tea towel and leave to rise in a warm, draught-free place until doubled in size – about 1½ hours.

Heat the remaining olive oil in a large pan, add the onions and cook for 10 minutes or until softened and lightly coloured. Add the tomatoes and cook gently until collapsed and very thick. Split the anchovies, remove the backbone, rinse and roughly chop. Stir into the sauce and season to taste.

Preheat the oven to 180°C (350°F) Gas 4. Knock back the dough, knead lightly, then stretch and pat it out into the prepared tin, pushing the dough well up the edges. Spread the sauce on top of the dough, cover with the whole garlic cloves and the olives, then sprinkle with the oregano. Drizzle with a little olive oil and bake for about 1 hour until golden. Serve sliced – hot, warm or cold.

½ recipe Basic Focaccia (page 16), making just 1 focaccia

3 tablespoons extra virgin olive oil

6 fresh ripe figs, quartered or sliced

6 slices prosciutto crudo

125 g/4 oz. Taleggio or Gorgonzola cheese, sliced

sea salt and freshly ground black pepper

Makes 1 focaccia, 25 cm/10 inches

This is just the thing to make when there are very good fresh figs around. The combination of sweet juicy figs, salty ham and rich, runny Taleggio is heady stuff. Mozzarella and Gorgonzola would both work well here (you need a soft melting cheese) and for a variation you can try making it with over-ripe peaches instead of figs.

stuffed focaccia with figs, prosciutto and Taleggio

Bake the focaccia without the rosemary following the recipe on page 16. Remove from the oven and tip out of the pan.

Holding the hot focaccia in a tea towel to protect your hands, slice through it horizontally with a serrated knife.

Brush the insides with the olive oil. Fill with the figs, prosciutto and Taleggio, seasoning as you go. Put the top back on and wrap loosely in aluminium foil, then return to the hot oven for 5 minutes. Unwrap, cut into thick wedges and eat whilst warm and melting.

Doesn't focaccia have to have dimples? Well, in general it does, but it varies depending on where you live in Italy. This recipe merits being called focaccia because it is made with an olive-oil enriched dough, and it has a filling, like so many focaccias. It's the Italian equivalent of bacon and egg pie, but it's made with lots of parsley and lovely fresh ricotta.

ricotta and Parma ham focaccia

½ recipe Basic Focaccia (page 16), making just 1 ball of dough, up to the first rising

4 eggs

6 tablespoons ricotta

6 tablespoons chopped fresh parsley or rocket/arugula

55 g/½ cup freshly grated pecorino cheese

150 g/5 oz. thinly sliced Parma ham

extra virgin olive oil, to glaze

sea salt and freshly ground black pepper

a pizza pan or springform cake pan, 23 x 4 cm/9 x 1½ inches, lightly oiled

Makes 1 focaccia, 23 cm/9 inches

Preheat the oven to 220°C (425°F) Gas 7 for at least 30 minutes.

While the dough rises, make the filling. Put the eggs, ricotta and parsley in a food processor and process until smooth. Pour into a jug and mix in the pecorino. Season with pepper but no salt.

Uncover the dough, punch out the air and knead until smooth. Roll two-thirds of it into a 32-cm/13-inch circle and use this to line the pizza pan, draping the extra dough over the edge. Alternate layers of Parma ham and ricotta mixture until they are all used up.

Roll the remaining dough into a 27-cm/11-inch circle. Brush the edge of the filled dough with water. Lift the circle of dough over the pie and press the edges to seal. Trim off the excess dough with a sharp knife. Brush with olive oil. Make 2 slashes in the centre of the pie. Bake for 20–25 minutes until golden. Serve warm or cold.

rustic focaccia with red pepper and onion

½ recipe Basic Focaccia (page 16), making just 1 focaccia, with 1 teaspoon dried basil added to the flour

Topping

3½ tablespoons olive oil

½ red pepper, deseeded and thinly sliced

½ red onion, thinly sliced

a 20 x 30-cm/8 x 12-inch baking sheet or tart pan, greased

Makes 8–10 portions

Light and simple, this flavoursome focaccia is great served to accompany soup and makes a tasty addition to any picnic basket.

Make the focaccia dough following the recipe on page 16, adding 1 teaspoon dried basil to the flour and leaving out the rosemary. Knead the dough and give it the first rising.

Uncover your mixing bowl and transfer the ball of dough to a well-floured surface. Knead well for a couple of minutes, then leave to rest for 5 minutes.

Roll out the dough with a rolling pin until big enough to fit your baking sheet. Transfer to the baking sheet and stretch it to fit snugly. Push your finger into the dough repeatedly to make dents about 2 cm/1 inch apart all over the surface.

For the topping, drizzle the oil evenly over the focaccia and scatter the pepper and onion over the top. Cover and leave to rest for another 40 minutes. It will increase in size again.

Preheat the oven to 200°C (400°F) Gas 6.

Uncover the focaccia and bake in the preheated oven for 15 minutes – it should be pale gold. Remove from the oven and leave to cool. Store in an airtight container or bread bag for up to 2 days.

This amazing focaccia features the reverse of dimpling – cobbles, which ooze cheese when they are cut open. The secret is to roll out the dough very thinly so that it hasn't got time to absorb the cheese.

oozing cheese focaccia

250 g/2 cups plus 2 tablespoons Italian '00' flour

6 tablespoons warm water

3 tablespoons extra virgin olive oil, plus extra to glaze

5 balls cow's milk mozzarella (*fior di latte*), or a smoked mozzarella, which will be firmer

6 tablespoons dried breadcrumbs

sea salt

a testo, terracotta bakestone or a large, heavy baking sheet

a rimless baking sheet

Makes 1 focaccia, 30 cm/14 inches

First, make an unleavened dough by mixing the flour, the warm water and the olive oil. Add more warm water if necessary. Knead well until smooth and elastic, then place in a bowl, cover and leave to rest for 1 hour.

Put the testo, terracotta bakestone or a large, heavy baking sheet on the lower shelf of the oven. Preheat the oven to 220°C (425°F) Gas 7 for at least 30 minutes.

Divide the dough into 2, making one piece slightly larger than the other. Using plenty of flour for dusting, roll the larger piece as thinly as you can into a 30-cm/12-inch circle directly onto non-stick baking parchment and slide onto a rimless baking sheet.

Cut the mozzarella balls in half and lightly squeeze out any moisture. Dip the bases in the dried breadcrumbs. Arrange the cheeses, domed-side up, over the pastry, adding any remaining breadcrumbs underneath each one. Roll out the remaining dough as thinly as you can and slightly larger than the base. Lift this over the cheeses and gently press the dough down and around each piece of cheese. The blunt edge of a biscuit cutter will help you to seal the edge of each mound – use a cutter that fits just around a mound. Make sure there are no holes for the cheese to run through. Twist and crimp the edges of the pizza together. Carefully brush with olive oil and sprinkle with salt.

Working quickly, open the oven door and slide paper and pizza onto the hot bakestone or baking sheet. If you are brave, try to shoot the pizza into the oven so that it leaves the paper behind – this takes practice!

Bake for 10–15 minutes or until golden, then remove from the oven and serve immediately, cut with a pizza wheel into oozing wedges.

focaccia alla diavola

This is a good, fiery focaccia for making sandwiches or serving in thick slices smothered in fresh ricotta. Replacing some of the liquid in the dough with tomato purée/paste (or even all the water with tomato juice) gives it a beautiful, rusty red colour, studded with bright red pepper and dark chunks of salami or chorizo.

½ recipe Basic Focaccia (page 16), making the changes stated in this recipe

4 tablespoons tomato purée/paste

4–6 red chillies or Peppadews, diced

2 red peppers, roasted, deseeded and diced

100 g/3½ oz. *salame piccante* or chorizo, cubed

75 g/2½ oz. *provolone piccante*, Emmental or Gruyère cheese, cubed

100 ml/⅓ cup extra virgin olive oil, plus extra to glaze

coarse sea salt or rock salt

a cake pan or pizza pan, 25 x 4 cm/10 x 1½ inches, lightly oiled

Makes 1 focaccia, 25 cm/10 inches

Make the focaccia dough following the recipe on page 16, but using 4 tablespoons tomato purée/paste dissolved in the water. Knead the dough and give it the first rising.

Uncover the dough, punch out the air and pull or roll it out into a rough circle. Dot with the chillies, red peppers, salami, provolone and lots of freshly ground black pepper. Flip one half of the dough over and lightly knead to incorporate the ingredients. Shape into a rough ball on a lightly floured surface and pat into the prepared tin. Cover lightly with clingfilm/plastic wrap or a damp tea towel and leave to rise for 30 minutes.

Remove the clingfilm and, using your fingertips, make deep dimples all over the surface of the dough. Drizzle over the olive oil, re-cover very lightly with clingfilm and leave to rise for a final 30 minutes until very puffy. Preheat the oven to 200°C (400°F) Gas 6.

Uncover the focaccia, mist with water and sprinkle generously with salt. Bake for 20–25 minutes until risen and golden. Transfer to a wire rack, brush with olive oil and leave to cool. Eat on the same day or leave to cool, then wrap up and freeze. When you remove it from the freezer, thaw and wrap in aluminium foil, then reheat for 5 minutes in a hot oven.

la marocca

500 g/4¼ cups Italian '00' flour

300 g/2¼ cups fine polenta flour (farina gialla or granoturco)

2 x 7-g/¼-oz. sachets/packages fast-action/quick-rising dried yeast

200 g/7 oz. black olives, pitted and halved

3 tablespoons pine nuts

2 tablespoons chopped fresh sage

2 tablespoons chopped fresh rosemary

2–3 garlic cloves, finely chopped

3 tablespoons extra virgin olive oil, plus extra to drizzle

450 ml/2 cups hand-hot water

rock salt and freshly ground black pepper

a Swiss/jelly roll pan, 33 x 23 cm/13 x 9 inches, oiled

Makes 1 focaccia, 33 x 23 cm/13 x 9 inches

This unusual focaccia from the coastal areas of Lunigiana is made from a mixture of cornmeal and wheat flour. It is traditionally made between November and the end of January to coincide with the olive harvest. It is cooked in a wood-fired oven on a bed of chestnut leaves, and takes on a deep brown crust. It must be eaten on the day, and is often served as part of an antipasto.

Mix the flours and yeast in a large bowl. Add the olives, pine nuts, sage, rosemary and garlic, then mix. Make a well in the centre and add the olive oil mixed with the hand-hot water. Mix to a very soft dough, turn out onto a lightly floured work surface and knead very vigorously for 10 minutes.

Roll or pull the dough into a rectangle to fit the Swiss/jelly roll pan, pushing the dough into the corners. Cover with clingfilm/plastic wrap or a damp tea towel and leave to rise in a warm place for about 20–30 minutes until quite puffy.

Meanwhile, preheat the oven to 200°C (400°F) Gas 6.

Using your fingertips, make deep dimples all over the dough and drizzle with olive oil. Sprinkle with salt and bake for about 35 minutes, until risen, firm and dark golden.

2½ teaspoons dried active baking yeast

1 teaspoon sugar

350–450 ml/1⅔–2 cups hand-hot water

125 g/1 cup fine oatmeal/oat flour, warmed

500 g/4¼ cups Italian '00' flour or plain/all-purpose unbleached white flour, warmed

2 teaspoons English mustard powder

1 teaspoon freshly ground black pepper

2 teaspoons fine salt

2 tablespoons extra virgin olive oil, plus extra to drizzle

3–4 tablespoons porridge/old-fashioned rolled oats

rock salt

two Swiss/jelly roll pans, 23 x 32 cm/9 x 13 inches, oiled

Makes 2 thin, rectangular focaccias

oat focaccia

Although not traditional, the addition of oatmeal to the Italian flour (and a sprinkling of porridge oats and salt on top) gives a thin, crisp, but still moist focaccia, with a golden, crunchy topping. Make sure all the ingredients are at warm room temperature, and if necessary, warm them in a low oven – this will help the dough to rise.

Whisk the yeast and sugar into the hand-hot water and stir in the warmed oatmeal/oat flour. Cover and leave to stand in a warm place for 10–15 minutes until frothy.

Sift the flour, mustard powder, pepper and salt into a warm bowl, pour in the oatmeal mixture and add the olive oil. Mix to a soft dough. Add a little extra warm water if the dough looks too dry. Turn out and knead for at least 10 minutes or until elastic (see page 15).

Place in a lightly oiled bowl, cover with clingfilm/plastic wrap or a damp tea towel and leave to rise in a warm place for about 1 hour or until doubled in size.

Uncover the dough, punch out the air and divide in 2. Pull and roll each piece to fit the Swiss/jelly roll pans. Place in the pans and press into the corners. Prick the dough all over with a fork and scatter the oatmeal flakes and salt over the top. Cover with oiled clingfilm or a damp tea towel and leave to rise until puffy – 30–60 minutes.

Preheat the oven to 200°C (400°F) Gas 6.

Drizzle the focaccias with olive oil and bake for 25 minutes until golden. Remove from the oven and drizzle with a little more olive oil. Cool on a wire rack and serve cut into thin fingers. Best eaten the same day.

truffled breakfast focaccia

Now here's something to start the day properly. Little warm focaccias are split, the insides brushed with a few drops of truffle oil mixed with melted butter, and filled with crispy fried pancetta and a fried egg. A real special-occasion dish. Be careful when you use truffle oil, as it can be overpowering; and be sure to use real truffle-infused oil, not the artificially flavoured variety.

½ recipe Basic Focaccia (page 16), making just 1 ball of dough, up to the first rising

4 tablespoons extra virgin olive oil, plus extra to fry

a few drops of good truffle oil

100 g/6½ tablespoons unsalted butter, melted

12 thin slices pancetta or streaky bacon

4 eggs

sea salt and freshly ground black pepper

4 deep, springform cake pans, 12 cm/5 inches each, lightly oiled

Makes 4 focaccias, 12 cm/5 inches

Uncover the dough, punch out the air and divide into 4. Shape each piece into a round ball on a lightly floured surface. Roll out into 12-cm/5-inch circles and place in the prepared cake pans. Cover with clingfilm/plastic wrap or a damp tea towel and leave to rise for 30 minutes. Preheat the oven to 200°C (400°F) Gas 6.

Using your fingertips, make deep dimples all over the dough right to the base of the pans and drizzle with the olive oil. Re-cover and leave to rise to the top of the pans – about 30 minutes.

Spray the focaccias with water, sprinkle generously with salt and bake for 20–25 minutes until risen and golden.

While the focaccias are baking, mix the truffle oil with the melted butter and keep warm. Grill the pancetta until crisp – or bake in the oven at the same time as the focaccia. Fry the eggs in olive oil and keep warm.

When the focaccias are ready, tip them out of their pans, hold them in a tea towel to protect your hands and slice through them horizontally with a serrated knife. (If they seem too thick, shave a slice off the inside.) Brush the insides with the truffle butter and lay three pancetta rashers and an egg on each one. Replace the tops and serve immediately.

To make the focaccias ahead of time, bake them and leave to cool, then wrap up and freeze. When you remove them from the freezer, thaw and wrap in aluminium foil, then reheat for 5 minutes in a hot oven.

These golden, puffy and delicious little flatbreads are made with fine cornmeal and wheat flour. They are similar to English muffins and are served at local *sagre* (festivals) in the Lunigiana, Tuscany.

cornmeal muffins

25 g/1 cake fresh/compressed yeast, 1 tablespoon dried active baking yeast or 2 teaspoons fast-action/quick-rising dried yeast

1 teaspoon sugar

400 ml/1¾ cups hand-hot water

500 g/4¼ cups Italian '00' flour

200 g/1⅔ cups fine cornmeal or polenta

1½ teaspoons fine sea salt

6 tablespoons extra virgin olive oil

a testo or heavy-based skillet or frying pan

Makes 8 muffins

In a medium bowl, cream the fresh yeast with the sugar and whisk in the hand-hot water. Leave for 10 minutes until frothy. For other yeasts, follow the manufacturer's instructions. Sift the flour, cornmeal and salt into a large bowl and make a well in the centre. Pour in the yeast mixture and the olive oil. Mix with a round-bladed knife, then your hands, until the dough comes together.

Tip out onto a lightly floured surface, wash and dry your hands (this will stop the dough sticking to them), then knead briskly for 5–10 minutes until smooth, shiny and elastic. Try not to add any extra flour at this stage – a wetter dough is better. If needed, flour your hands and not the dough. If it is really too soft to handle, knead in a little more flour. To test if the dough is ready, roll it into a fat sausage, take each end in either hand, lift it up and pull the dough outwards, gently wiggling it up and down – it should stretch out quite easily. If not, it needs more kneading.

Shape into a neat ball. Place in an oiled bowl, cover with clingfilm/plastic wrap or a damp tea towel and leave to rise in a warm, draught-free place until doubled in size – about 1½ hours. Heat the testo or heavy-based frying pan on the stove until medium hot.

Uncover the dough, punch out the air, then tip out onto a lightly floured surface. Divide into 8 smooth balls, then flatten each into a disc about 1 cm thick. Slide 2 or 3 discs onto the hot testo or frying pan and cook for about 2 minutes on each side, until risen and deep brown on the underside.

Keep the cooked muffins warm and soft in a cloth or loosely wrapped in aluminium foil in a warm oven. They are best served warm. Serve split and filled with cheese, alongside a selection of cold meats and salami.

Making a bread by mixing mashed potato with flour and anointing it lavishly with good olive oil is common all over Italy, especially in Liguria and Puglia, where some of the best olive oil comes from.

potato and olive focaccia

450 g/1 lb. baking potatoes, unpeeled

625 g/5¼ cups Italian '00' flour

½ teaspoon fine sea salt

25 g/1 cake fresh/compressed yeast, 1 packet active dried baking yeast, or 2 teaspoons fast-action/quick-rising dried yeast

180 g/6½ oz. large, juicy green olives, pits in

150 ml/⅔ cup extra virgin olive oil

coarse sea salt

two cake pans, 25 x 4 cm/ 10 x 1 ¾ inches each, lightly oiled

Makes 2 focaccias, 25 cm/10 inches

Boil or bake the potatoes in their skins and peel them whilst still warm. Mash them or pass them through a potato ricer.

Sift the flour with the fine salt into a large bowl and make a well in the centre. Crumble in the fresh yeast, or add dried yeast, if using. If you are using dried yeast, follow the manufacturer's instructions. Add the potatoes and mix together with your hands until the dough comes together. Tip out onto a floured surface, wash and dry your hands and knead energetically for 10 minutes until smooth and elastic. The dough should be soft; if it isn't, add a couple of tablespoons warm water.

Divide the dough into 2, shape each piece into a round ball on a lightly floured surface and roll out into two 25-cm/10-inch circles or a large rectangle to fit whichever pan you are using. Put the dough in the pan, cover with clingfilm/plastic wrap or a damp tea towel and leave to rise for 2 hours.

Preheat the oven to 200°C (400°F) Gas 6. Uncover the dough, scatter over the olives, and, using your fingertips, make deep dimples all over the surface of the dough, pushing in some of the olives here and there. Drizzle with two-thirds of the olive oil, re-cover and leave to rise for another 30 minutes.

Uncover the dough, spray with water and sprinkle generously with salt. Bake for 20–25 minutes until risen and golden brown. Brush or drizzle with the remaining olive oil then transfer to a wire rack to cool. Eat on the same day, or leave to cool, then wrap up and freeze. When you remove the focaccia from the freezer, thaw and wrap in aluminium foil, then reheat for 5 minutes in a hot oven.

25 g/1 cake fresh/compressed yeast

200 ml/¾ cup hand-hot water

a pinch of sugar

4 eggs (at room temperature), beaten

500 g/4¼ cups Italian '00' flour

100 g/1 cup freshly grated Parmesan cheese

sea salt and freshly ground black pepper

relish or pesto (page 20), to serve

a ring mould, 23 cm/9 inches, oiled and dusted with flour

Makes 1 ring, 23 cm/9 inches

Easter cheese focaccia

This unusual cheese loaf is baked in a ring mould because the dough is made from a loose batter – almost a brioche – and the mould will hold it nicely. This sort of bread is normally only made for holidays and celebrations, but it's delicious toasted for breakfast; the smell will rouse even the sleepiest member of the household. The bread can easily be baked in a loaf pan but it is not quite as pretty.

Dissolve the yeast in the hand-hot water with the sugar. Whisk in the eggs. Put the flour and Parmesan in an electric mixer and season. Pour in the yeast mixture and mix slowly, on a low setting, for 5 minutes until smooth. Turn up to medium and mix for a further 5 minutes. The batter should be very soft. Pour or scoop the batter into the prepared ring mould, cover with a damp tea towel and leave to rise for 1 hour or until puffy.

Preheat the oven to 180°C (350°F) Gas 4.

Bake the dough in the oven for 35–40 minutes until well risen and a deep, rich brown on top. Invert onto a wire rack and leave to stand for 10 minutes in the mould. Lift off the mould, turn the bread over and cool. Serve, in slices, with relish or pesto.

chestnut and Vin Santo focaccia

500 g/4¼ cups Italian '00' flour or plain/all-purpose white flour

200 g/1⅔ cups chestnut flour (*farina di castagne*)

1 teaspoon fine sea salt

25 g/1 cake fresh/compressed yeast, 1 tablespoon dried active baking yeast or 2 teaspoons fast-action/quick-rising dried yeast

150 ml/⅔ cup extra virgin olive oil

150 ml/⅔ cup Vin Santo mixed with 300 ml/1⅓ cups water, warmed

rock salt, to sprinkle

2 cake pans, pie or pizza pans, 25 x 4 cm/10 x 1½ inches, lightly oiled

Makes 2 focaccias, 25 cm

Mixing wheat flour with chestnut flour gives this focaccia a wonderful sweet and savoury flavour – almost smoky. It is generally made during the autumn/fall or winter months when chestnut flour is available and at its best. Serve it with lovely runny Gorgonzola and fresh pears as a dessert – with extra Vin Santo to sip.

Sift the flours and salt into a large bowl and make a well in the centre. Crumble in the fresh yeast. For other yeasts, follow the manufacturer's instructions. Pour in 3 tablespoons of the olive oil, then rub into the yeast until the mixture resembles fine breadcrumbs. Pour the Vin Santo and water into the well and mix together until the dough comes together.

Tip out onto a lightly floured surface, wash and dry your hands (this will stop the dough sticking to them), then knead briskly for 10 minutes until smooth and elastic. The dough should be very soft, almost too soft to handle, but don't worry at this stage. Put in a lightly oiled bowl, cover with clingfilm/plastic wrap or a damp tea towel and leave to rise in a warm place until doubled – about 1½ hours.

Uncover the dough, punch out the air, then divide into 2. Shape each piece into a round ball on a lightly floured surface. Roll out into 25-cm/10-inch circles and put in the pans. Cover with clingfilm or a damp tea towel and leave to rise in a warm place for about 45 minutes or until very puffy and almost risen to the top of the pans.

Uncover the dough and, using your fingertips, make deep dimples all over the surface of the dough right to the base of the pan. Drizzle over the remaining oil, re-cover and leave to rise for a final 30 minutes. Preheat the oven to 200°C (400°F) Gas 6.

Spray the focaccias with water, lightly sprinkle with rock salt and bake for 20–25 minutes until risen and golden. Transfer to a wire rack to cool. Eat on the same day or leave to cool, then wrap up and freeze. To reheat, thaw and wrap in aluminium foil, then heat for 5 minutes in a hot oven.

black grape schiacciata

This is a delicious bread to serve warm from the oven at breakfast time. This recipe uses fresh black grapes, but it can also be made successfully using semi-dried Montepulciano grapes. If you wanted to try something similar, you could substitute semi-dried cherries or plump Lexia raisins.

80 ml/⅓ cup extra virgin olive oil

a handful of fresh rosemary needles

450 g/3½ cups strong white bread flour

1 teaspoon fine sea salt

2 tablespoons caster/superfine sugar

1 teaspoon fast-action/quick-rising dried yeast

250 ml/1 cup hand-hot water

400 g/14 oz. seedless black grapes

a deep baking pan, oiled

Makes 1 medium loaf

Put the olive oil and rosemary in a bowl. Give the rosemary several good squeezes to release the aroma into the oil. Set aside for a few minutes.

Put the flour, salt and 1 tablespoon of the sugar in a large bowl and stir well. Add the yeast and stir again. Pour in 2 tablespoons of the infused, strained olive oil and enough hand-hot water to make a soft but not sticky dough.

Turn the dough out on to a lightly floured work surface and knead for 5 minutes, until the dough is smooth and elastic. Fold in the grapes and knead for a further 2–3 minutes. The dough may become sticky at this point, so dust with a little extra flour if necessary.

Press the dough into the prepared baking pan and push it with your knuckles to fill the tin. Leave to rise in a warm place for about 40 minutes, or until it has doubled in size. Preheat the oven to 220°C (425°F) Gas 7.

Drizzle the remaining infused olive oil over the risen dough and scatter some of the rosemary needles and the remaining sugar evenly across the top. Bake for about 25 minutes or until the surface is golden brown and the base sounds hollow when tapped. Cool on a wire rack.

Eat on the same day or let cool completely, wrap in foil and freeze. When you remove the bread from the freezer, thaw and wrap in foil, then reheat for 5 minutes in a hot oven.

sweet Easter focaccia

This focaccia, enriched with egg and butter and infused with saffron, once symbolized wealth and generosity. The dough needs time to rise – the more sugar, butter and eggs in it, the longer it takes. Let it rise slowly in the fridge overnight for the main rising, or even the final proving.

25 g/1 cake fresh/compressed yeast, 1 tablespoon dried active yeast, or 2 teaspoons fast-action/quick-rising dried yeast

1 large pinch saffron threads or 2 small sachets powdered saffron

150 g/¾ cup sugar

200 ml/¾ cup hand-hot water

450 g/3¾ cups Italian '00' flour

1 teaspoon salt

5 egg yolks

finely grated zest of 1 unwaxed orange and 1 unwaxed lemon

150 g/10 tablespoons unsalted butter, softened

1 egg, beaten

100 g/1 cup whole blanched almonds

icing/confectioners' sugar, to dredge (optional)

a shallow cake pan, 25 cm/10 inches, oiled

Makes 1 focaccia, 25 cm/10 inches

Put the yeast and saffron into a large measuring jug and add a teaspoon of the sugar. Mix well, then pour in the hand-hot water and whisk until the yeast is dissolved. Leave in a warm place for 10 minutes until frothy.

Whisk 100 g/¾ cup of the flour into the yeast mixture to make a thick, smooth batter. Cover with clingfilm/plastic wrap and leave to rise in a warm place for about 1 hour until doubled in size. (This could be done overnight in the fridge.)

Sift the remaining flour and salt into the bowl of a food mixer. Add the remaining sugar, egg yolks, orange and lemon zest, and beat until well mixed. Pour in the batter and beat until smooth and elastic – about 5 minutes. Cover the bowl with clingfilm and leave to rise in a warm place until doubled in size – about 2 hours.

Remove the clingfilm and gradually beat in the soft butter until shiny and elastic – another 5 minutes. The dough will be very soft. Tip out onto a lightly floured board and shape into a smooth ball. Transfer this to a sheet of baking parchment and roll out into a disc about 2.5 cm/1 inch thick. Cover with an upturned bowl and leave to prove for 1 hour or until puffy, or, put the dough in the cake pan and leave to prove in the pan.

Preheat the oven to 180°C (350°F) Gas 4. Once the dough has risen, brush it lightly with the beaten egg, and lightly push the almonds randomly into the surface. Bake for 1 hour until risen and golden. Serve dredged with icing/confectioners' sugar, if using, and with dessert wine.

Pizzette are small or bite-size pizzas. In Italy they are often served in bars to enjoy with your 'aperitivi'. Here you'll find easy recipes for pizzette and other tasty savoury bites made using both pizza and focaccia doughs.

pizzette and small bites

Pizza dough

½ x 7-g/¼-oz sachet/package or 1 ½ level teaspoons fast-action/quick-rising dried yeast

250 g/2 cups plain/all-purpose flour

½ teaspoon fine sea salt

5 tablespoons olive oil

175 ml/⅔ cup hand-hot water

Toppings

1 small aubergine/eggplant, thinly sliced

1 onion, thinly sliced

pinch of fresh thyme leaves

4 generous teaspoons sun-dried tomato paste

75 g/½ cup cherry tomatoes, quartered

125 g/4 oz. dolcelatte or Gorgonzola cheese, crumbled

8 slices of pepperoni

handful of black olives

100 g/3½ oz. mozzarella, diced

2 teaspoons basil pesto

2 canned artichoke hearts, sliced

2 tablespoons semi-dried tomatoes

handful of wild rocket/arugula

sea salt and freshly ground black pepper

fresh basil leaves, to garnish

solid baking sheet

Makes 4 mini pizzas

This selection of mini pizzas has four deliciously different toppings – aubergine/eggplant and dolcelatte; pepperoni, mozzarella and olives; artichoke, semi-dried tomato and pesto; and sautéed onions with dolcelatte. Perfect for sharing with friends and a bottle of wine.

mini pizzas

To make the pizza dough, mix together the flour, yeast and salt in a large bowl. Add 2 tablespoons of the olive oil and the water and mix to a soft dough. Lightly dust the work surface with flour, tip the dough out of the bowl and knead for 5 minutes, or until smooth and elastic. Shape the dough into a neat, smooth ball, return to the bowl and cover with clingfilm/plastic wrap. Leave in a warm place for 1 hour, or until doubled in size.

Heat 2 tablespoons of the oil in a frying pan and fry the aubergine/eggplant on both sides until golden, then remove from the heat. In another pan, heat the remaining olive oil and gently fry the onion until very tender and just starting to turn golden. Add the thyme and remove from the heat.

Preheat the oven to 230°C (450°F) Gas 8. Divide the dough into 4 evenly sized pieces and shape each piece into a pizza about 15 cm/6 inches in diameter. Place on a solid baking sheet, then spread sun-dried tomato paste over 2 of the pizzas. Top one pizza with the aubergine slices, cherry tomatoes and half the crumbled dolcelatte. Top the other pizza with pepperoni, olives and half the diced mozzarella.

For the third pizza, spread the basil pesto over the base and arrange the artichoke hearts and semi-dried tomatoes on top. Scatter the remaining mozzarella over it. Garnish with basil leaves. Top the last pizza with the sautéed onions and remaining dolcelatte. Season all the pizzas well with salt and pepper and cook on the top shelf of the oven for about 5 minutes, or until golden. Top the onion pizza with the rocket/arugula and serve immediately.

½ recipe Basic Pizza Dough (page 13), making just 1 ball of dough

6 tablespoons Classic Pesto Genovese (page 20)

small goats' cheese log with rind (300 g/10 oz.)

4 fat garlic cloves, thinly sliced

extra virgin olive oil, to glaze

sea salt and freshly ground black pepper

a round biscuit cutter, 7 cm/3 inches (optional)

Makes 12 pizzette

goats' cheese and pesto pizzette

The variety of goats' cheese to use here is the one with a snowy white rind that will hold its shape in the oven – just cut the pizza bases to fit the sliced cheese. Coupled with freshly made pesto, this is a marriage made in heaven. The pizzette are perfect served with drinks, as they can be assembled ahead of time and cooked at the last moment. If you make them beforehand, prick the bases all over to prevent them from rising too much, add the toppings, then cover and refrigerate until ready to cook.

Preheat the oven to 220°C (425°F) Gas 7.

Uncover the dough, punch out the air and roll or pull very thinly on a well-floured surface. Using an upturned glass or a biscuit cutter, stamp out twelve 7-cm/3-inch circles and lay on a lightly oiled baking sheet. Alternatively, cut the circles of dough to match the size of your goats' cheese log. Spread the pizzette with a little pesto.

Slice the goats' cheese into 12 slices and lay a slice on top of the pesto. Arrange a couple of slices of garlic on the goats' cheese and brush with olive oil. Season and bake for 8–10 minutes or until the cheese is beginning to melt. Serve immediately.

little fried Neapolitan pizzas

½ recipe Basic Pizza Dough (page 13), making just 1 ball of dough

½ recipe Pizzaiola Sauce (page 18)

1 buffalo mozzarella, squeezed of excess water, then cut into tiny sticks

12 fresh basil leaves

vegetable or olive oil, for deep-frying

a round biscuit cutter, 5 cm/2 inches (optional)

a wok or deep fat fryer

Makes about 12 pizzas

These crisp little circles of fried pizza topped with a blob of tomato sauce, cool white mozzarella and fresh basil are often served in bars in Naples with your *aperitivi*. Although best served straight from the pan, you can make the puffy pizza crusts beforehand, let them cool, and store in an airtight container. To reheat, put them in a warm preheated oven for 2 or 3 minutes, then add toppings and serve.

Uncover the dough, punch out the air and roll or pull very thinly on a well-floured surface. Using an upturned glass or a biscuit cutter, stamp out 12 or more 5-cm/2-inch circles.

Heat the oil in a wok or deep fat fryer to 190°C (375°F) or until a tiny piece of dough sizzles instantly when dropped in. Fry the pizzas, 4 at a time, for 2–3 minutes or until puffed and golden. You will have to turn them now and again so that they colour evenly. Remove with a slotted spoon and drain on kitchen paper.

Top with a little pizzaiola sauce, a stick of mozzarella and a basil leaf. Serve immediately whilst still hot.

little Tuscan pizzas

Schiacciate ('skee-a-chah-tay') in Tuscany are individual thin, crispy pizzas with the simplest of toppings. The dough is rolled out to almost baking-parchment thinness, laid on an oiled baking sheet, then topped with cheese, vegetables and prosciutto, all of which are cut wafer-thin so that they will cook quickly. Mozzarella is often used as the base instead of tomato sauce, and sliced fresh tomatoes or halved cherry tomatoes are scattered on top of the cheese. Fresh herbs or a handful of peppery rocket/arugula are often added when the pizza comes sizzling out of the oven.

1 recipe Basic Pizza Dough (page 13)

Choose from the following toppings (thinly slice any vegetables and mozzarella):

salami, red onion and capers

aubergine/eggplant, red onions, mozzarella and sage

potato, mozzarella, anchovy, olive, sage or rosemary

courgette/zucchini, mozzarella, anchovy and basil

mozzarella, tomato and rocket/arugula

extra virgin olive oil, to drizzle

sea salt and freshly ground black pepper

2 heavy baking sheets

Makes 6 small, thin pizzas

Place 2 heavy baking sheets in the oven. Preheat the oven to 220°C (425°F) Gas 7 for at least 30 minutes.

Uncover the dough, punch out the air and divide into 6. Shape each piece into a smooth ball and roll into a very thin circle. Put the discs on a couple of baking sheets lined with non-stick baking parchment. Arrange a few slices of mozzarella on top (if using). Toss the chosen sliced vegetables in a little olive oil and arrange sparingly on top of the pizza bases along with any other toppings.

Working quickly, open the oven door and slide paper and pizzas onto the hot baking sheets. Bake the pizzas for 15–20 minutes, or until the crust is golden and crisp. Remove from the oven, scatter with any herbs, drizzle with olive oil and serve immediately.

Almost like little muffins, these tiny treats hide a surprise when you bite into them – a tomato bathed in pesto and melting mozzarella. Make them in advance and reheat in a warm oven.

little stuffed focaccia muffins

½ recipe Basic Focaccia (page 16), making just 1 ball of dough, risen twice but uncooked

8 tablespoons Classic Pesto Genovese (page 19)

24 small cherry tomatoes

1 cow's milk mozzarella (*fior di latte*), squeezed of excess water, then diced

sprigs of thyme or rosemary, to decorate

rock salt

a round biscuit cutter, 7 cm/3 inches (optional)

two 12-hole mini-muffin pans, oiled

Makes about 24 muffins

Preheat the oven to 200°C (400°F) Gas 6.

Uncover the dough, punch out the air and divide the dough into 4. Roll or pull each piece as thinly as you can on a well-floured work surface. Using an upturned glass or a biscuit cutter, stamp out 6 little circles. Place a scant teaspoon of pesto in the middle of each circle, add a little mozzarella, then top with a cherry tomato. Bring the sides up and over the tomato and pinch to seal.

Put the muffins, sealed-side down, in the prepared mini-muffin pans. Brush the tops with olive oil, push in a herb sprig and sprinkle with rock salt. Bake in the oven for 10–15 minutes until risen and cooked through. Tip out of the pans and eat warm, as a snack, with drinks.

500 g/4¼ cups strong white bread flour

1 x 7-g/¼-oz. sachet/package or 3 level teaspoons fast-action/quick-rising dried yeast

1 teaspoon fine sea salt

4 tablespoons extra virgin olive oil

300 ml/1¼ cups hand-hot water

2 tablespoons fresh rosemary leaves

2 generous teaspoons sea salt flakes

Garlic mushrooms

1 tablespoon olive oil
1 tablespoon unsalted butter
1 shallot, finely chopped
250 g/8 oz. mixed wild mushrooms
1 tablespoon chopped parsley
1 garlic clove

Mediterranean tomatoes

4 ripe tomatoes
1 roasted red pepper, from a jar
1 tablespoon mixed pitted olives
1 tablespoon fresh basil leaves, torn
100 g/3½ oz. buffalo mozzarella, torn

Beans and mint

175 g/1⅓ cups broad/fava beans
1 tablespoon freshly chopped mint
grated zest of ½ unwaxed lemon
100 g/3½ oz. feta, crumbled
1 garlic clove

*baking pan,
20 x 30 cm/8 x 12 inches*

Serves 4–6

assorted focaccia crostini

Focaccia is one of the tastiest breads to make, and so easy that it's a crime not to bake it yourself, and it can be made in advance.

Mix together the flour, yeast and fine salt in a large bowl. Add 1 tablespoon of the olive oil and the water and mix to a soft dough. Lightly dust the work surface with flour, tip the dough out of the bowl and knead for 10 minutes, or until smooth and elastic. Shape the dough into a neat, smooth ball, return to the bowl and cover with clingfilm/plastic wrap. Leave in a warm place for 1 hour, or until doubled in size. Lightly oil the baking pan. Dust the work surface with flour, tip the dough out and knead for 30 seconds. Roll the dough into a rectangle to fit in the baking pan. Lay the dough inside the pan. Cover with oiled clingfilm and leave in a warm place for about 1 hour, or until doubled in size. Preheat the oven to 220°C (425°F) Gas 7. Dimple the dough with your fingertips, drizzle the remaining olive oil all over it and scatter the rosemary and salt flakes over the top. Bake in the preheated oven for about 20 minutes, or until golden brown and well risen. Let cool in the pan for about 10 minutes, then transfer to a wire rack. Cut the focaccia into finger-width slices, toast both sides on a ridged stovetop griddle/grill pan and top with one of the following toppings. Serve warm.

For garlic mushrooms, heat the oil and butter in a frying pan, add the shallot and cook over medium heat until translucent. Add the mushrooms, season, cook until tender and stir through the parsley. Rub the garlic clove over the toasted bread and pile the mixture on top. Drizzle with olive oil.

For Mediterranean tomatoes, chop the tomatoes, red pepper and olives. Add the basil and olives and gently stir through the mozzarella. Rub the garlic clove over the toasted bread and pile the mixture on top. Drizzle with olive oil.

For beans and mint, cook the beans in lightly salted boiling water until tender. Drain and refresh under cold water. Drain well, then whiz in a food processor to a coarse purée. Stir in the mint, lemon and feta and season. Rub the garlic clove over the toasted bread and pile the mixture on top. Drizzle with olive oil.

½ recipe Basic Pizza Dough
(page 13), making just 1 ball
of dough

100 g/3½ oz. smoked mozzarella
cheese, cut into small cubes

100 g/3½ oz. *salame piccante*
or chorizo, diced

200 g/¾ cup ricotta

60 g/⅔ cup freshly grated
Parmesan cheese

3 tablespoons chopped
fresh basil

vegetable or olive oil, for
deep-frying

sea salt and freshly ground
black pepper

*a round biscuit cutter,
8 cm/3 inches (optional)*

a wok or deep fat fryer

Makes about 15 panzerotti

Panzerotti or 'little fat bellies', from the Italian *pancia*, meaning 'tummy', are a great favourite in southern Italian pizzerias. The filling is usually some type of salami and cheese, and they can be quite large. They puff up like swollen bellies when deep-fried.

panzerotti

Mix together the mozzarella, salami, ricotta, Parmesan and basil. Season.

Uncover the dough, punch out the air and roll or pull very thinly. Using an upturned glass or a biscuit cutter, stamp out about 15 little circles.

Place large spoonfuls of the filling onto one half of each pastry circle. Fold the other half over, pinching well to seal, then neaten the edges with a fluted pastry cutter.

Heat the oil to 190°C (375°F) in the wok or deep fat fryer and deep-fry the panzerotti in batches until puffed, crisp and brown. Flip them over to cook both sides evenly. Drain on kitchen paper and season with salt. Serve immediately while still warm and gooey.

Parmesan fritters

½ recipe Basic Pizza Dough
(page 13) or Sicilian Pizza Dough
(page 14), making just 1 ball
of dough

8 tablespoons freshly grated
Parmesan cheese, plus extra
to dust

vegetable or olive oil, for
deep-frying

a round biscuit cutter (optional)

a wok or deep fat fryer

Makes about 16 fritters

Here's another quick snack made from leftover pizza dough, and
often served in bars. All you need is some fresh Parmesan cheese
and you've got a delicious appetite-whetter. Just don't eat too many!

Uncover the dough, punch out the air and roll or pull as thinly as you
can, flouring the surface well. Using an upturned glass or a biscuit cutter,
stamp out as many circles as you can – you can make them any size.
Place a little mound of Parmesan in the centre of each one and fold
in half, pinching the edges together.

Heat the oil in the wok or deep fat fryer to 190°C (375°F). A piece of
stale bread dropped in should sizzle and turn golden in a few seconds.
Fry in batches until puffed and golden on both sides. Drain well on kitchen
paper, then toss the fritters in some grated Parmesan. Serve hot.

pancetta and fennel puffs

These *coccoli* ('little darlings') are a type of savoury doughnut or *bomboloni* flavoured with pancetta. Lightly crushed fennel seeds are added, a flavouring that is very popular in Tuscany, especially with cured pork. They are deep-fried until crisp on the outside and soft inside and can be kept warm in the oven. Make sure they are piping hot and sprinkled liberally with sea salt when you serve them. Grind fennel seeds over them for a special finishing touch.

200 ml/¾ cup milk

50 g/1¾ oz. pure lard, roughly chopped

40 g/1½ cakes fresh/compressed yeast or 1 sachet/package fast-action/quick-rising dried yeast

400 g/3½ cups Italian '00' flour

50 g/1½ oz. pancetta, finely diced

1 teaspoon fennel seeds, lightly crushed

vegetable or olive oil, for deep-frying

sea salt

a deep fat fryer

Makes 30–40 puffs

Put the milk and lard in a saucepan and heat gently until the lard has melted. Don't let the milk get too hot. Crumble in the fresh/compressed yeast (if using) and whisk until dissolved. Sift the flour and a good pinch of salt into a bowl and make a well in the centre. If you are using fast-action/quick-rising dried yeast, stir it into the flour now. Pour in the warm milk mixture, and add the pancetta and fennel seeds. Mix to a soft dough, adding more flour if necessary. Form into a ball, cover with clingfilm/plastic wrap or a damp tea towel and leave to rise for 2 hours or until doubled in size.

Heat the oil in the deep fat fryer to 180°C (350°F). A piece of stale bread dropped in should sizzle and turn golden in a few seconds.

Uncover the dough, punch out the air and knead for 1 minute. Pull off small walnut-sized pieces of dough, about 2 cm/¾ inch, and roll into rough balls. Fry in batches for about 2–3 minutes until pale brown and puffy. Drain well and tip onto kitchen paper. Sprinkle with salt and serve while still hot.

walnut and parsley rolls

1 recipe Basic Pizza Dough
(page 13)

200 g/1 ½ oz. walnut pieces

a handful of fresh parsley leaves

2 garlic cloves

100 ml/⅓ cup extra virgin olive oil

sea salt and freshly ground
black pepper

*a deep pizza pan or springform
cake pan, 23 cm/9 inches,
lightly oiled*

Makes about 20 small rolls

These are delicious little savoury rolls made just like Chelsea buns
and baked together in a pan. Take the whole lot to the dinner table
and break off your own little roll. Perfect with drinks on a hot summer
night, or instead of bread, they disappear very fast!

Preheat the oven to 200°C (400°F) Gas 6.

Put the walnuts, parsley and garlic in a food processor and process
until evenly chopped. While the machine is running, pour in the olive
oil. Season to taste.

Uncover the dough, punch out the air and roll or pull into a rectangle,
60 x 20 cm, directly onto a large sheet of non-stick baking parchment.

Spread the walnut mixture over the dough. Season. Using the parchment
paper, roll the dough up like a Swiss/jelly roll, starting from the long side.
Slide the dough onto another sheet of parchment making sure the seam
is underneath. Using a large and very sharp knife cut the roll into 20
even pieces. Cut the dough quickly and smoothly each time – don't saw
it or it will stick! Arrange the rolls cut-side up in the prepared pizza pan,
spacing them close together but not quite touching. Cover with oiled
clingfilm/plastic wrap or a damp tea towel and leave to rise to the top
of the pan for about 30 minutes.

Remove the clingfilm and bake the rolls for 35–45 minutes or until
golden. Leave to cool in the pan if you want them very soft, or turn
them out onto a rack to cool if you'd like them drier. Serve warm.

Who doesn't love bread dough? But often the dough balls in pizza restaurants are just too heavy. Here little balls of pizza dough are washed with a salty glaze. Try splitting them while they are hot, pulling out the doughy centre and filling with ricotta, a spoonful of aubergine/eggplant antipasto and some good canned tuna in oil.

dough balls

1 recipe Basic Pizza Dough (page 13) or Sicilian Pizza Dough (page 14)

1 tablespoon fine sea salt

ricotta, marinated aubergine/ eggplant and tinned tuna, to serve (optional)

a large baking sheet lined with parchment paper

Makes 10–12 balls

Preheat the oven to 200°C (400°F) Gas 6.

Uncover the dough, punch out the air and divide it into 12. Shape each piece into a neat ball.

Put the dough balls on the prepared baking sheet, spacing them well apart. Cover loosely with lightly oiled clingfilm/plastic wrap or a damp tea towel and leave to rise again until doubled in size – about 30 minutes.

Dissolve the salt in 3 tablespoons water. When the dough balls have risen, brush them with the salt solution.

Bake the rolls for 15–20 minutes until risen and browned. Cool on a wire rack then split and fill with the ricotta, aubergine/eggplant and tuna.

index

photography credits

key:
a=above, b=below, r=right,
c=centre, background=bkgrd

Steve Baxter
Pages 41, 120, 131

Martin Brigdale
Pages 15bc, 24, 51, 63, 75,
87, 110 insert

Peter Cassidy
Pages 2, 5, 15a, 15b, 18,
25, 30, 37 insert, 46, 69, 70
insert, 77 bkgrd, 78 insert,
90, 95, 98 insert, 126, 110
bkgrd, 114 bkgrd, 118, 126
bkgrd

Tara Fisher
Page 129 insert

Richard Jung
Pages 1, 3, 4, 10–14, 17, 19
all apart from bkgrd, 21, 22,
27, 28, 29 insert, 31, 32, 33,
35, 36, 40, 43, 44, 47, 48,
52, 55, 59, 60, 62, 64, 67,
68, 71, 72, 76, 79, 80, 84,
88, 91, 92, 94, 96–97, 99,
100, 103, 104, 107, 108,
110 bkgrd, 111, 112, 115,
116, 117 insert, 119, 123,
124, 126 insert, 127, 128,
132, 134 insert, 135, 136,
139, 140

Sandra Lane
Page 38

Lisa Linder
Pages 7, 34

William Lingwood
Pages 39, 57 insert

Steve Painter
Pages 8, 9 all, 16, 23, 61,
73, 82, 83, 117 bkgrd,
129 bkgrd

William Reavell
Pages 20, 29 bkgrd,
42 insert, 49, 50, 65, 66,
81, 85, 122, 125

William Shaw
Page 77 insert

Debi Treloar
Page 15br, 114 insert

Kate Whitaker
Pages 6, 19 bkgrd,
26, 37 bkgrd, 42 bkgrd,
45, 53, 54, 56, 57 bkgrd,
58, 70 bkgrd, 74, 78 bkgrd,
86, 89, 93, 98 bkgrd, 101,
102, 105 bkgrd, 106, 109,
113, 121, 130, 133, 134
bkgrd, 137, 138, 141–144

Polly Wreford
Page 105 insert

recipe credits

All recipes by Maxine Clark with the following exceptions:
page 26 Fiona Beckett, page 38 Silvana Franco, page 86
Ross Dobson, page 94 Isidora Popovic, page 114 Liz Franklin,
pages 120 and 130 Annie Rigg